Creative
Backstitch

Creative
Backstitch

Helen Hall

Guild of Master Craftsman Publications Ltd

First published 2002 by
Guild of Master Craftsman Publications Ltd,
166 High Street, Lewes,
East Sussex BN7 1XU

Reprinted 2003

ISBN 1 86108 251 7
A catalogue record of this book is available from the British Library
Photographs by Christine Richardson
Illustrations by Carrie Hill, based on sketches by Richard Hall

Designed by John Hawkins
Cover design by John Hawkins
Typefaces: ITC Novarese and Monotype Gill

Colour origination by Viscan Graphics (Singapore)
Printed and bound by Kyodo Printing (Singapore)

This book is dedicated to the memory of my
mother, Sheila Irene Cousins. Without her support and
encouragement during the early days of my design work,
I would never even have contemplated the possibility
of offering my designs for publication. Her death was not
only a great loss to myself and all my family, but also to
everyone whose life she touched, however inadvertently,
and we all miss her so very much. I feel it is such
a shame that she did not live long enough to see the
results of her encouragement as I am sure she
would have thoroughly enjoyed this book.

I would like to thank my son Richard for taking time
out of his AS coursework to do the rough sketches for
the illustrations so that Carrie had something
to work from, and my daughter Nicola for her endless
help with my computer disasters. Also, I would like
to thank my editor Lindy Dunlop for her boundless
enthusiasm and commitment, which has resulted
in this book being finished much earlier than
I had, at first, anticipated.

Contents

Introduction

Many people have learnt a few basic stitches in school needlework classes; running stitch, backstitch, cross stitch, even chain stitch. What I want to do is show that you don't need to be a genius to create things; using just one simple stitch type, in this case backstitch, you can work beautiful designs. Patterns using just one stitch have a beauty in their simplicity, and the added advantage of being quicker and easier to complete.

Of course, I hope you like the designs in their original state but if you don't, my aim is to show how to alter and adapt them to suit your own purpose. After all, haven't we all seen a project that we would love to stitch but simply don't have room for another picture, coaster or whatever. I hope you will feel confident enough to change the designs, if you want to, in order to make something you really would love to keep, or give to someome special.

Chapters 1 and 2 cover the tools and materials used and the reasons why I think they are the best for these particular projects. Chapters 3 to 7 include small, quick projects that can be finished in a couple of days or so. These vary in complexity, so experienced stitchers will still have something to get their teeth into. Guidelines for each give a rough indication of how long they may take to complete, and of their level of difficulty. Chapter 8 contains one larger project and Chapter 9 shows how to adapt designs, or one section of a design, for different uses.

Part One
Tools and materials

1 | *Working the design*

In order to complete the projects in this book, you will need some specialist materials and tools. To help you make sure you have everything you need, I have put together some notes on the materials and equipment available, and listed those that I have used for the projects in this book.

MATERIALS

Fabrics

Stitchwork that requires the even spacing of stitches (known as counted threadwork) is best carried out on materials with an even weave, that is, materials that have an equal number of evenly spaced warp (vertical) threads and weft (horizontal) threads. Such materials are usually referred to by their count – the number of threads that can be counted, in either direction, to the square inch. I have used Aida for all the projects in this book. Aida is a type of evenweave fabric, described as a blockweave because of its appearance. As with all evenweaves, Aida has the same number of threads in each direction, but they are woven into blocks, which creates clearly visible holes. This manner of weaving makes the material quite firm and, therefore, less likely to distort than some of the other evenweave materials, such as linen. With Aida, the count refers to the number of holes in each direction, rather than the number of threads.

Fig 1.1
Aida is available in a wide range of colours; these are all 14 count

Fig 1.2
Compare the weave of these 28-count fabrics (the lavender and white are Annabelle and the pink is a country-style evenweave) with that of the blockweave Aida in Fig 1.1

Fig 1.3
Aida is also available in ready-made bands; useful for bookmarks and decorative edgings

My choice

I have used 14-count Aida for all the designs as it is the most readily available and the easiest to work with, if you want to make items of a manageable size. However, if you prefer to work on a different count, there is no reason why you shouldn't. Just remember that a higher count will produce a smaller finished design and a lower count a larger one. Equally, you can substitute any other type of evenweave material, but do remember that a looser weave is more prone to distortion and don't pull your stitches too tight or you may ruin your finished piece.

Threads

Stranded cotton floss

There are many different types of thread available nowadays, making this a much cheaper hobby than it was when there was only finely spun silk. The most popular choice for ordinary counted threadwork is stranded cotton floss as it is versatile – you can use it in different thicknesses and for both embroidery and general stitching – and offers a huge range of colours. It is most readily available in a six-stranded form. Cutting this into suitable lengths, ideally not longer than 40cm (16in), will allow you to separate the strands and remove the number you need without too great a risk of knotting.

Fig 1.4
The strands of cotton floss can be separated to give the thickness of thread you require

Metallic embroidery thread

Stranded metallic embroidery thread is good for adding sparkle to a design, but its colour range is somewhat limited. As each strand of a metallic thread is very fine, to give a particular thickness, a greater number of strands are required than with ordinary cotton floss. These threads also tend to be quite slippery which can make it difficult to keep your needle threaded.

Fig 1.5
Stranded metallic thread can be more difficult to work with than cotton floss

A good alternative to using all metallic threads is to combine one strand of ordinary cotton floss with one or two strands of metallic. In this way you get a touch of sparkle without it completely dominating the design. The addition of a little metallic thread can enhance any design but don't go overboard with it unless you are after a very showy piece. Experiment with combining colours; a darker or lighter shade of cotton floss will make the metallic thread stand out while a contrasting colour will give a more dramatic effect. Some manufacturers make spools of metallic blending threads that are specifically designed for use with cotton floss. Spools of blended metallic cord, with many threads twisted or woven together, are also available in different thicknesses and a good selection of colours. When working in this type of backstitch, it is best to use a fine cord or you will lose definition in more complex designs.

Fig 1.6
(Right) Metallic blending threads are designed to be used with cotton floss

Fig 1.7
(Far right) A little metallic thread can enliven a design and add a sense of celebration

Perlé cotton

Perlé cotton is a two-ply thread – it is not stranded and therefore should not be split. Perlé is a little more lustrous than ordinary stranded cotton. It is available in a number of thicknesses; again, for this type of backstitch, choose a fine thread, especially when working more detailed designs.

Fig 1.8
As perlé cottons are not stranded, you need to buy a thread in the thickness you require

Rayon threads

Rayon threads will give your work a lovely sheen without making it too glitzy. It used to be available only in spools of single-stranded thread, but some manufacturers now produce six-stranded versions as well. This makes it easier to get the right balance when you are using it in place of, or blending it with, cotton floss. As it is a little thicker than stranded cotton, I would recommend varying the number of strands you use according to the intricacy of a particular area of a design; for more complex designs, use just one strand.

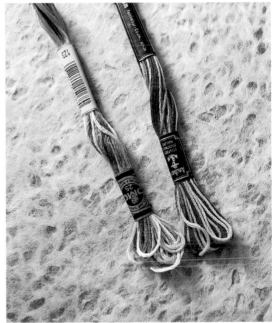

Variegated threads

Many manufacturers offer variegated or 'space-dyed' threads in a number of their ranges. These work extremely well with the technique used in this book: the colour fades in and out beautifully as the pattern is worked.

Fig 1.9
(Above left) Rayon threads are now available in stranded and unstranded forms

Fig 1.10
(Above right) Variegated threads look beautiful even in their skeins

Fig 1.11
In a finished design, the variegation is more subtle

My choice

I have used six-stranded cotton floss for most of the designs in this book because of its excellent colour range, availability and reasonable price. However, some of the pieces in Chapter 9 (see pp 112 and 113) show how much difference a simple change of thread type or colour can make.

EQUIPMENT

Needles

To stitch the designs you need a blunt tapestry needle, size 24 or 26. The blunt 'point' of these needles make it easier to stitch cleanly through the holes without splitting the fabric, which would result in uneven stitches and spoil the effect of your work.

Fig 1.12
The blunter end of tapestry needles reduces your chances of splitting the weave of the fabric as you stitch

Scissors

You need a pair of fabric shears or dressmaking scissors, to be used solely for cutting the fabric to size, and a pair of small, sharp, pointed embroidery scissors for cutting and trimming the thread; the pointed ends are also useful for unpicking your work should you be unfortunate enough to make a mistake. If you do have to use them for this purpose, be very careful not to cut the strands of the fabric as well. It helps to place your needle under the stitch and lift it away from the fabric a little so that you can slide the point of the scissors under the thread cleanly before you cut. It is important that you use the embroidery scissors only for this type of work if you want to keep them sharp. If you use them for cutting other items (particularly paper), they will soon become blunt and will no longer cut through thread cleanly.

Fig 1.13
You will need both embroidery scissors and fabric shears for your work

Fig 1.14
Rolling frames make it easier to keep your fabric stretched taut

Frame

The use of a frame is a matter of personal preference. Most of the projects in this book are small enough not to need one though the chessboard (see p 98) and the cushion made using the adapted chessboard design (see p 122) would both be difficult to complete without one: it would be impossible to keep the tension correct while working these dense designs over such a large area.

I have found that the best type of frame for this sort of work is a rolling frame. These are rectangular frames with rollers at the top and bottom. After pinning or tacking your fabric to these rollers, you simply turn them to take up the fabric until it is stretched tight and then lock them in place by tightening the fastenings. Rolling frames are available in various widths. To complete the chessboard or cushion cover you will need one at least 50cm (20in) wide.

Using pins

If you pin your fabric to the frame, you must not leave it stretched taut for extended periods or the pinheads will distort it. You should also check the rollers regularly to make sure that none of your pins have come loose. If they do fall out your tension will be altered, and you might have the painful experience of treading on one.

TECHNIQUES

Getting started

The first thing you need to do is cut your fabric to size. Aida is easy to cut in a straight line as you can simply follow a line of holes. The size required is given at the start of each project.

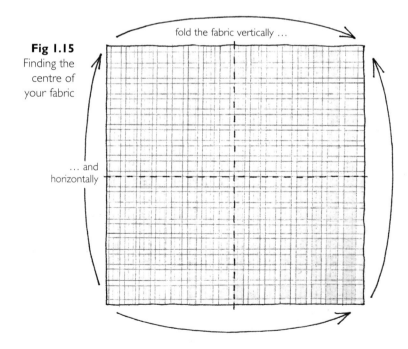

Fig 1.15
Finding the centre of your fabric

fold the fabric vertically …

… and horizontally

Finding the centre

Once you have cut your fabric to size you need to find its centre (see Fig 1.15). Counted threadwork is always stitched from the centre outwards: as there are no guidelines or patterns printed on the fabric, it is important to be sure that your finished design will be central. To find the centre, fold the fabric in half in one direction, then in half again from the other direction; the hole at the point where the folds cross is the centre.

Adjustments for central blocks

If you find a block at the centre point instead of a hole, don't worry, simply move to one of the holes surrounding it. You may need to trim a line of blocks from one side of the design to even up the edges once you have finished the stitching, but that is all.

It is a good idea to mark the centre so that you don't lose your place. If the design is small and you are ready to start stitching straight away, you can simply slip a pin into the hole. However, if the design is large and repetitive, like the chessboard, it is best to mark it in a more permanent and obvious way. Tie a large knot at one end of a good length of brightly coloured thread, making sure it isn't a colour

end of thread
tied in a bow

Fig 1.16
Marking the centre with a thread bow

you'll be using for the design. Thread a needle with this and draw it through the centre hole, leaving a length remaining on the right side of the fabric. Remove the needle then tie a bow in the thread on the right side. This will mark the centre of your design, you will not be able to pull it out by mistake, and you can simply move it to one side when you need to stitch into the centre hole. When you want to remove the thread, untie or cut the bow and pull it out from the back of the fabric. Try to avoid stitching through your marker thread or you won't be able to do this when the time comes.

To find the centre of the graph, draw one line – in your mind or in light pencil on the paper – to join the top and bottom arrows and another to join the side arrows; the centre is where they cross. If the design has no stitch at the centre, count outwards to the first stitch shown on the graph, in whatever direction this may be, then mirror your actions on the fabric; this will be your starting point.

Starting and finishing threads

Avoid using knots to start or finish a thread as they will create lumps in your work and will spoil the look of the finished item. To start off the first thread, insert your needle from the back of the fabric, and draw the thread through, leaving about 2cm (¾in) on the reverse side. Hold this 'tail' against the fabric and work a few stitches of the design over it (see Figs 1.17 and 1.18).

Fig 1.17
(Right) To start a thread, hold the 'tail' flat on the fabric …

Fig 1.18
(Far right) … and work a few stitches over it to secure

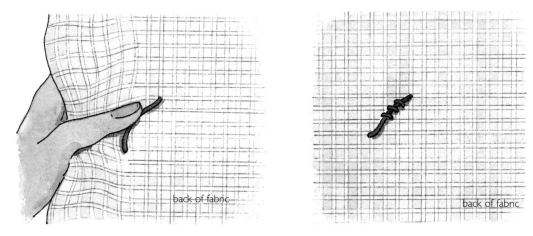

Once you are sure it is secure, begin the design and continue stitching until you have about 5cm (2in) of thread left in your needle. At this point, push the needle through to the back of the fabric and turn your work over. Work your needle under and over the last few stitches you worked to secure the thread (see Fig 1.19), then remove the needle and trim back any excess.

Start and finish all threads in this way. Try not to start and finish too many threads in the same area as this will create lumps in your work in much the same way as a knot would.

Fig 1.19
(Right) Weave your needle through the last few stitches at the back of the design to fasten off

Fig 1.20
(Far right) To work one backstitch, bring your needle up at 1, take it down at 2, then up again at 3

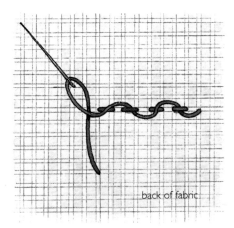

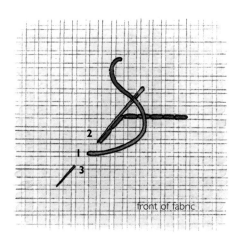

Backstitch

In this book, the only stitch used in the designs is backstitch (see Fig 1.20). One stitch on the graph represents one block on the fabric – the distance between each hole. Backstitch is quick and easy, even for a complete beginner.

Washing and pressing your work

You should always work with clean hands and avoid situations in which your work could be spoilt by dirt or spillages. However, if you have been working on a project for a long time and it has become stained or dirty due to bad storage or accidents (ideally, you should store your work in a bag to protect it from dirt, spillages, and abrasive damage), you may need to wash it. Hand wash the item in lukewarm water with a small amount of mild hand soap. Never wash your work in a washing machine, never use detergents and never scrub the fabric or stitching: machine washing will damage the surface of both the stitching and the fabric as it is quite harsh; many detergents are either acidic or alkaline and will eat into the fabric; and if you scrub the finished item you will damage the stitching and the fabric. It is also important not to have the water too hot or the colours may run. If this does happen, don't panic, just keep rinsing the item in cold water until the water runs clear and the runs have disappeared.

After washing, always rinse your work thoroughly to remove all traces of soap: If any soap remains, it may eventually eat into the fabric, as soap rarely has a neutral pH value. When you are satisfied that it is clean, gently squeeze out any excess water, then roll the piece up in a clean towel. Squeeze the towel to remove as much of the remaining water as you can – it is OK to twist the towel gently as you are doing this – then unroll and reshape the piece as necessary.

Lay your work face down on a clean, dry towel, folded to provide extra padding, then carefully finish the drying with a medium-hot iron; dab the iron onto the fabric rather than dragging it over the surface as this can cause distortion. Continue until your piece is completely dry.

Fig 1.21
Roll your work up in a towel before gently squeezing to remove excess water

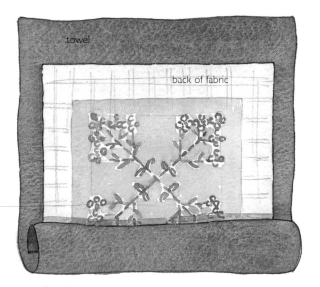

towel

back of fabric

2 | *Making up the finished piece*

When you are satisfied that your completed project is clean and dry, it is time to make it up into the finished article. Specific instructions for making up individual items are given at the end of each chapter, but I have listed any items that you may not have to hand here so that you can assemble everything you need before you start – this will save you time and avoid much unnecessary frustration.

MATERIALS

Felt

I use felt as a backing material to hide the stitching on the reverse side of my finished pieces. Felt, made from pressed wool, is a versatile, non-fraying fabric and is available in a good range of colours. This allows you to match, complement or contrast the backing of your finished article with the Aida or thread you have used. Baize can be used in the same way, but it lacks the colour range and thickness of felt, which helps to hide any odd lumps in your work.

Fig 2.1
Versatile felt can be used for padding as well as backing designs

I also use felt on projects for which I need just a little padding and for which even the lightest weight wadding would be too thick, as with the card designs.

Interfacing

Interfacing is available in different weights (light, medium and heavy) and in iron-on or stitch-on varieties. I use medium-weight, iron-on interfacing on small projects, such as coasters, that need to be cut back to fit into an aperture. This prevents the Aida from fraying. Interfacing also makes it possible to trim off the tiniest amounts of fabric in order to ensure a snug fit.

Fig 2.2
Iron-on interfacing
will prevent your
fabric fraying

Hemming webbing and bonding sheets

Iron-on hemming webbing is a mesh-like tape that is used to bond separate layers of fabric. A similar material, Bond-a-Web, is available in sheet form; this is useful when fusing larger pieces of fabric. I use hemming webbing in place of glue for fixing felt to the reverse side of an item. Using glue for this purpose has three disadvantages; it causes the fabrics to stiffen, it often bleeds through fabrics, which ruins the design, and, as it would dissolve or weaken in water, it means that the finished item cannot be washed.

Fig 2.3
Hemming webbing
and bonding sheets
allow you to fix
layers of fabric
together without
affecting their feel

Fig 2.4 (Top left) A selection of the author's home-made 'round' braid

Fig 2.5 (Top right) The advantage of making your own braid is that you can match the colours exactly to those used in the design. These samples are half-round

Fig 2.6 (Centre left) Flat braid is useful for covering the raw edge of a design

Fig 2.7 (Centre right) Commercial metallic braid is not suitable for edging

Fig 2.8 (Right) Ribbon can be used in place of braid

Braid

I use braid for finishing off, sometimes to cover raw edges and sometimes purely for decorative purposes. I make my own braid so you won't find exactly what is shown in this book in the shops. However, there is a good range of manufactured braiding available these days, and you could always use ribbon instead. If you'd like to try making your own braid, I would recommend *Beginner's Guide to Braiding: The Craft of Kumihimo* by Jacqui Carey. This excellent book provides all the information you need to start Japanese braiding, though you will also need some specialist equipment.

Lace

I use double-edged, slotted lace on projects with a drawstring top, such as the tubular scented sachets. It is easy to thread braid or ribbon through the slots or under the fold in the lace, and the braid can then be pulled up and knotted or tied in a bow to close the finished piece. If you want to open it again, simply untie and loosen the braid. I sometimes use gathered lace as a trimming, either on its own or together with braid. This is very effective on square, scented sachets, especially if you are going to display them.

Fig 2.9
(Below left) Thread ribbon through slotted lace to make a simple drawstring fastening

Fig 2.10
(Below right) Trim your piece with gathered lace for a decorative finish

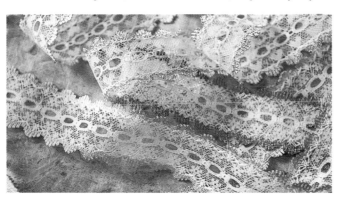

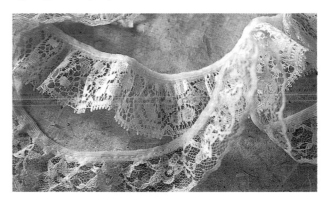

Wadding and fillings

Wadding is another item that comes in different weights. In its flat form It is ideal to pad out the designs of framed items: this helps disguise any small lumps or bumps that may have developed during the stitching process without you realizing. Lightweight polyester wadding is the most suitable for this purpose as it is thick enough to do the job but not so thick that it makes the framing process difficult.

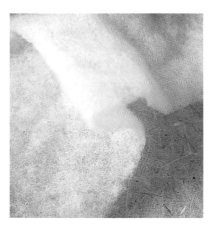

Fig 2.11
Wadding is now available in many weights; this is the lightweight form

It is best to stuff cushion covers with a ready-made cushion insert, as this will enable you to remove it for washing purposes, but there is nothing to stop you making your own insert or simply stuffing the cover with filling. Flame-retardant, polyester toy fillings are ideal for stuffing pincushions.

Mount board

Mount board is used to back pieces that are to be framed: if you tried to frame the fabric without mounting it, it wouldn't be stiff enough to stay in place and would gradually slide down into the frame. Stretch the unstitched fabric of the finished piece over the board, pin in place, lace to secure (see Figs 8.1–8.5 on pp 103 and 104), then insert the mounted work into the frame. It is very important to use only acid-free mount board as the acid in ordinary cardboard will gradually eat into the fabric and ruin your work.

Self-adhesive tape

I use a plastic-coated, self-adhesive fabric tape on the back of picture frames to cover the gap where the backboard fits into the actual frame. This seals the frame and protects the work from insects, moisture and dirt. Self-adhesive paper tape is also suitable but, over time, this tends to dry out and fall off the frame, leaving your work susceptible to the very dangers it was supposed to protect it from.

Double-sided tape

This tape is useful for holding two items together; I often use it to hold small designs, such as those used in cards, in place. Double-sided tape is sold in rolls and is available in various widths. To use it, all you need do is cut off the length you need, position it carefully, then peel off the backing. It is then simply a matter of carefully setting the second layer of the project in place. Make sure you have positioned the layers correctly before you attempt to stick them together: this type of adhesive tape has a very strong gluing action and it is difficult to remove items from it once they have been pressed into place, particularly those made from paper or card.

Fabric stiffener

This is a safe, non-toxic liquid and is best applied with a small paintbrush, like those found in children's paint sets. I use it where there is no room for a hem and in other situations where I need to stop fabrics fraying beyond a certain point, most often when I'm making a fringed edge, as for the pincushions, scented sachets and bookmarks included in this book. When fabric stiffener dries, it acts like glue and sticks the threads of the fabric together, so it is unable to fray.

Cards

All the cards I use are three-fold cards with apertures. They are fairly easy to get hold of and a lot less trouble than making them yourself, though if you have the time, skill, and necessary equipment, you can save quite a bit of money by doing so.

Lavender

I have used lavender for the scented sachets because I grow it myself, so it is easy for me to harvest and dry it, but there is no reason why you shouldn't use any pot-pourri, as long as it is a dry mix: a wet mix would eventually cause the fabric to become mouldy. Try different combinations depending on the time of year, and if the item is to be a present for someone, fill it with their favourite pot-pourri mix.

Fig 2.12 The scent of lavender is known to have a calming effect

If you want to try drying lavender yourself, here are a few tips:

- Do not cut lavender when the flowers are wet or they will go mouldy before they have a chance to dry out
- Try to cut the stem as long as possible as this makes it easier to tie the stems in bunches
- Tie the stems into small bunches: air might not circulate very well around the central flowers in a big bunch so they might not dry, and if they start to go mouldy the whole bunch will be ruined
- Hang these upside down in a warm, dry place (ideally an airing cupboard or somewhere similar): if you tried to hang the bunch from the flowers, a very difficult task, the bunch would fall as the dried flowers came away from the stalk
- Secure a paper bag around the flower heads as individual flowers may fall off during the drying process; this creates a mess and leaves the flowers unusable

In these conditions, it normally takes about two weeks for the flowers to dry. It is easy to check if they are ready; simply remove the bag and rub your finger and thumb down the flower spike, against the direction of the growth. If the individual flowers feel hard and crisp and come away from the stem easily, the drying process is complete; if not, replace the bag and hang the bunch up for another few days.

To harvest the flowers, follow the same procedure as testing for dryness. Store them in an airtight container, away from direct sunlight, to preserve their scent.

EQUIPMENT

Scissors
You will need embroidery scissors for trimming back fabrics.

Needles
You will need a sharp sewing needle to stitch up some of the projects, though a tapestry needle would be fine where you are stitching two layers of Aida together by matching the holes.

TECHNIQUES

Running stitch

I have used running stitch (see Fig 2.13) to make up some of the projects in this book. As with the backstitch, each stitch on the graph represents one block on the fabric.

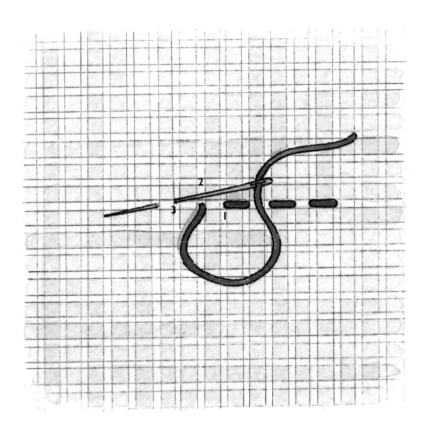

Fig 2.13 To work one running stitch, take your needle down at 1, up at 2, then down at 3

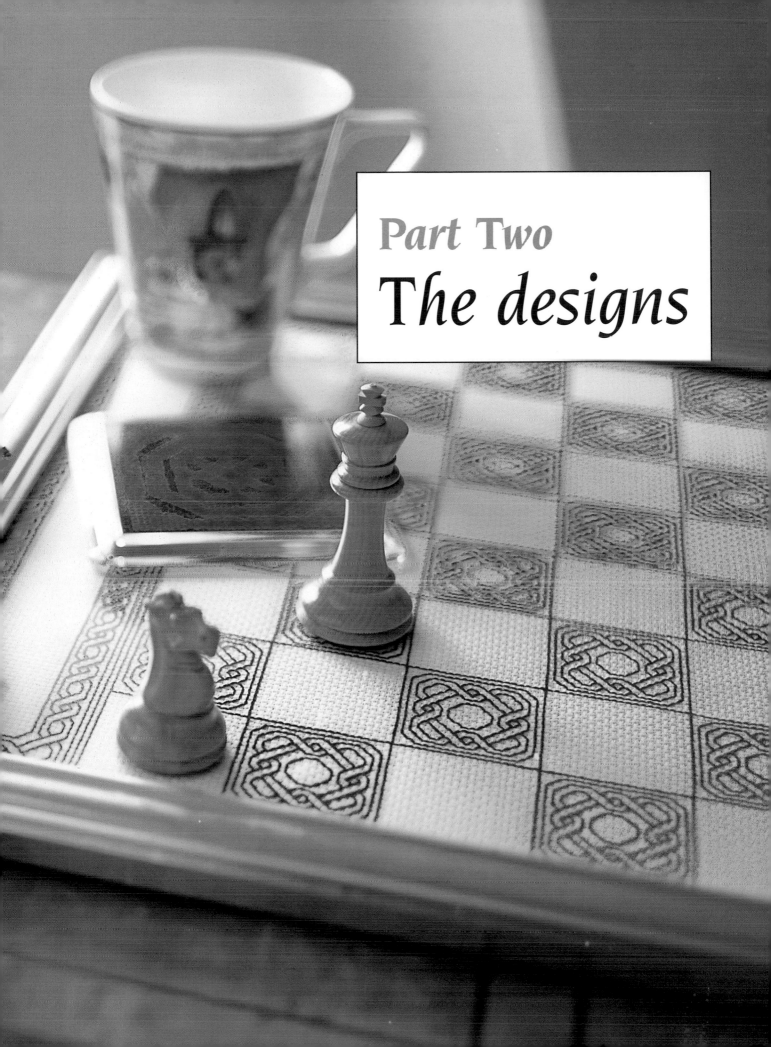

Part Two
The designs

3 | Bookmarks

In this world of computer technology, many have said that the day of the conventional book is nearly over, but I do not agree. I am sure that the enjoyment of books will continue for some time yet, so I have put together a small collection of bookmarks.

All of the projects in this chapter use two strands of cotton floss. The design sizes and amounts of thread given are approximate.

Electric-blue bookmark

⊠⊠ *Skill level* Intermediate

⊠⊠ *Average completion time* Two to three days

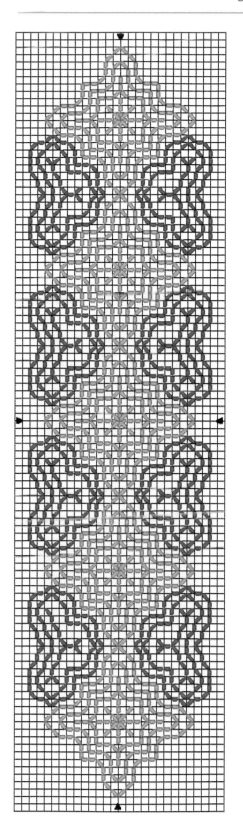

Design size
4 5 × 17.5cm (1¾ × 7⅛in)

Stitch count
24 × 100

Fabric
Zweigart Aida, 14 count, black
6 × 25cm (2¼ × 10in)

Threads required

		Anchor	DMC	Madeira	Amount
	Electric-blue, medium	433	996	1103	1m 50cm (5ft)
	Electric-blue, dark	410	995	1102	1m 25cm (4ft)

Green band bookmark

⊠⊠⊠ *Skill level* Experienced
⊠⊠⊠ *Average completion time* Three to four days

Design size
5 × 20cm (1⅞ × 7⅞in)

Stitch count
27 × 110

Fabric
Zweigart Aida band, 14 count,
white edged with green
5.1 × 25cm (2 × 10in)

Threads required

		Anchor	DMC	Madeira	Amount
■	Christmas green, very dark	923	699/ 909	1302/ 1303	4m 10cm (13ft 6in)

Brown-and-cream bookmark

☒   *Skill level* Beginner

☒☒   *Average completion time* Two days

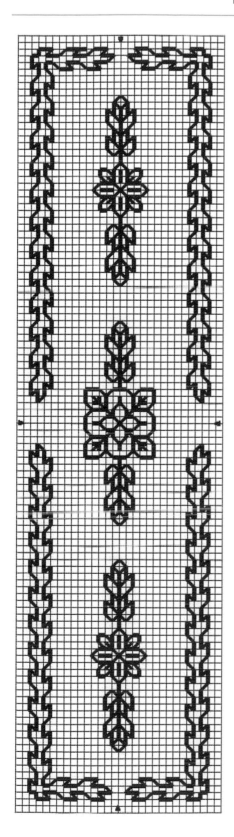

Design size
5 × 20cm (1⅞ × 7⅞in)

Stitch count
27 × 110

Fabric
Zweigart Aida band, 14 count, cream
5.1 × 25cm (2 × 10in)

Threads required

		Anchor	DMC	Madeira	Amount
■	Black-brown, very dark	382	3371	2004	2m 7cm (7ft)

Celtic bookmark

☒ *Skill level* Beginner

☒☒ *Average completion time* Two days

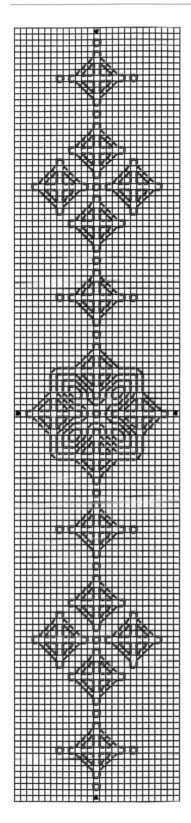

Design size
4 × 22cm (1⅝ × 8¾in)

Stitch count
24 × 123

Fabric
Zweigart Aida, 14 count, ivory
6.25 × 27.5cm (2½ × 11in)

Threads required

	Anchor	DMC	Madeira	Amount
Turquoise, dark	No equiv.	3812	No equiv.	1m 60cm (5ft 6in)

Red star bookmark

☒☒ *Skill level* Intermediate

☒☒ *Average completion time* Two to three days

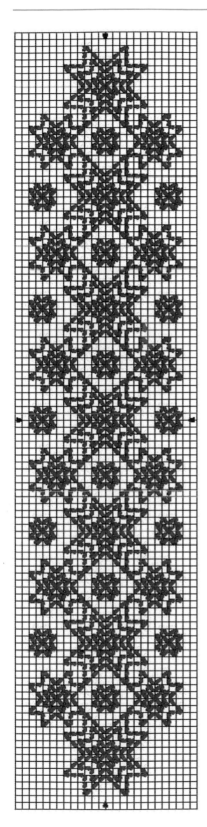

Design size
4 × 19.5cm (1⅝ × 7¾in)

Stitch count
23 × 108

Fabric
Zweigart Aida band, 14 count,
white edged with red
5.1cm × 25cm (2 × 10in)

Threads required

		Anchor	DMC	Madeira	Amount
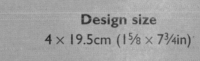	Christmas red, light	46	6662	0210	1m (39in)

Making up bookmarks

If your work needs washing, follow the instructions given in Chapter 1 (see p 17). If not, just follow the instructions for pressing (see p 17).

FROM AIDA BANDS

> **Tools and materials**
> Felt, 5cm (2in) × length of design
> Iron-on hemming webbing × 3 lengths, length of design
> Embroidery scissors
> Fabric stiffener
> Tapestry needle
> Towel
> Iron

Fig 3.1
Applying the
three lengths
of hemming
webbing

back of fabric

strips of hemming webbing

Place your work face down on a clean towel and lay the three lengths of hemming webbing side by side along the length of the design, on the reverse side of the fabric. It doesn't matter if these lengths overlap each other, but they musn't go past the edge of the design area; this includes the unsewn area at the top and bottom of the band. Lay the felt on top, taking care not to disturb the hemming webbing as you do so.

With your iron on a medium-hot setting, press it repeatedly onto the assembled layers. Do not drag it over the felt or you may cause it to pucker and bond with the Aida with creases set in it. It doesn't take very long for the fabrics to fuse, but it is quite easy to miss a small area, so it is essential that you check they have fused over their entire area before you continue. If they have, switch off your iron and leave it to cool, and move your Aida band to a clean, firm surface.

Using embroidery scissors, carefully trim back any excess felt from the scalloped edges of the band. Do this a little at a time to avoid cutting through the scalloped edging itself. When you have finished trimming the sides, trim across the top and bottom edges, but don't cut too closely to the design or you may find that the stitching shows under the edge.

Finishing off

Now is the time to decide how to finish the ends off. Whatever method you choose, it is a good idea to brush a little fabric stiffener along the row of blocks just beyond the edge of the stitched area, and leave it to dry. This will help to prevent the fabric fraying into the design. You could finish off by simply cutting the Aida back to just before the row of blocks you painted with fabric stiffener. Your bookmark would then be ready to use straight away.

Fringes

You may prefer to fringe your bookmark, as I have done with many of mine. This is also quite a simple procedure. The first step is to ensure that the top and bottom fringes will be the same length. To do this, count the number of holes at each end; if one end has more than the other, simply trim back the longer end until it has the same number as the shorter one. When you remove some of the horizontal threads from the band, you will find that the remaining vertical threads form a fringe. Use the point of your tapestry needle to loosen the first horizontal thread nearest the raw edge and pull it clear.

Fig 3.2 Loosening a thread with the sharp end of a tapestry needle

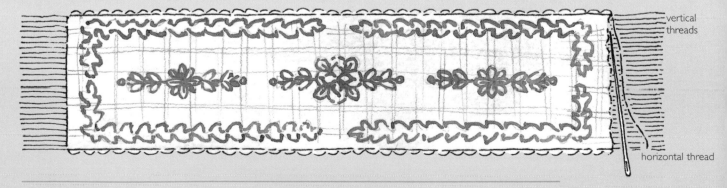

vertical threads

horizontal thread

Working with Aida bands

Some bands have an interlocking thread running along the length of one side to prevent excessive fraying. There is no way of identifying whether your band has this until you start removing threads, but if it does, each time you reach it, your progress will be halted. Cut it back as you go, but be careful not to cut into the fringe itself.

You may find that you have to remove a couple of threads that have been cut through before you reach a point where you have a continuous thread but once you do, you will be able to gently pull this until you have the length of fringe required. Be careful not to tangle the fringing threads as you work; this can cause the fabric to pucker and spoil your work. It could also lead to you removing more threads than you want to, through pulling the tangled length too hard. It is best to keep at least one row of blocks between the stitched area and the fringe – if you get any closer than this, your stitching will come undone.

When you have finished creating your fringe, cut off the threads that formed the scalloped edging as close as you can to the point where you have ended your fringing. As these threads are thicker than the vertical threads of the Aida band, they will spoil the look of the fringe even if they are the same colour. Once you have trimmed both ends, your bookmark is ready to use.

FROM CUT AIDA

Materials
Felt, same length and width as Aida used for design
Iron-on hemming webbing, 3–4 lengths, same length as felt
Braid × 2, approx. 10cm (4in) longer than Aida
Cotton floss to match colour of braid
Embroidery scissors
Sharp sewing needle
Tapestry needle
Stiff paper

If you are using a flat braid that is wide enough to fold over the raw edge of the Aida and still enable you to stitch through both layers of braid and the fabric at the same time, apply the hemming webbing as for bookmarks made with Aida band, then cut the top and bottom ends of your Aida at an angle to form a point. This looks best if you follow a diagonal line of holes from the edge of the Aida to the centre point on each side. Next, fold a length of braid over the edge of the fabric along one side of the design and pin it in place; ensure that the raw edge of the Aida is completely covered, and leave a 5cm (2in) length of braid at each end; this will be used to form the tassels.

5cm (2in)
extra braid

raw edge
of fabric

Fig 3.3 Pinning
the braid in place

If you are using a more rounded braid that will only cover the raw edge of the fabric at the front of the bookmark, shape the top and bottom points of your Aida and stitch the braid in place (remembering to leave a 5cm (2in) length of braid at the top and bottom of the Aida) *before* applying the hemming webbing and felt. The felt backing will cover the stitches on the reverse.

Using an ordinary sewing needle, stitch the braid in place with small running stitches; these can easily be hidden in the depth of the braid. Make sure each stitch goes through the fabric and both edges of the folded braid or you will end up with a little gap showing between the braid and the Aida.

Tassels

Cut two 15–20cm (6–8in) lengths of suitably coloured cotton floss; do not separate the strands. Wind one length tightly around the two loose lengths of braid at one end of the bookmark, as close to the pointed end of the fabric as possible. Make sure you wind it tightly over the cut end of the thread so that it can't come undone. When you have bound these securely, thread a tapestry needle with the free end of the floss, pass this under the thread you have just wound around the braid (the 'binding') on the reverse side of your work, and pull it tight. Fasten off by threading the needle under and over this 'binding' several times until you are sure that the thread will not work loose, then cut off any excess thread as close to the binding as possible.

Fig 3.4
Securing the
end of a tassel

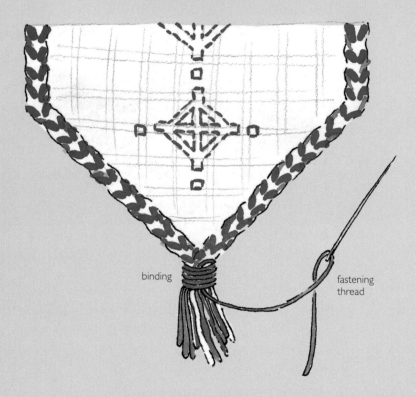

binding

fastening
thread

To form the tail of the tassel, unravel the braiding that extends beyond this binding. If the threads of the tail are curly and you would prefer them straight, try steaming them over the spout of a kettle or a pan of boiling water, then pulling them straight. Be careful not to scald yourself while doing this and never let children attempt it. Don't hold your hands directly over the steam; hold the tassel so that only the tail is over it. If the steam does scald you, hold your hand or fingers in cold water until the stinging subsides.

To make the ends of the tail threads neat and even, wrap a piece of stiff paper tightly around the tassel, close to the binding, and slide it down the tassel until the bottom edge is level with the shortest threads in the tail. With your embroidery scissors, carefully snip off any ends that protrude from the paper, then remove the paper and give the tassel a little shake to allow the tail threads to fall into place naturally.

Repeat this procedure to make the tassel at the other end of your bookmark, and it will then be ready to use.

Finishing without braid

If you prefer, it is possible to make these bookmarks without any braid. However, in this case, you must ensure that your bonding webbing and felt reach right to the edge of the Aida. You can trim them back if you have an uneven number of blocks along the sides around the design area, but it is advisable to add a little fabric stiffener to the edge of the Aida to reduce the chances of the fabric fraying.

4 | Coasters

If there's one thing you can never have too many of, it's coasters. It doesn't seem to matter how many you have or how cleverly you think you've placed them, someone will always manage to put a glass, mug, or cup and saucer on your freshly polished table top and damage it. I hope this collection of designs for round and square coasters will both enhance and protect your furniture in the future.

All the projects in this chapter use two strands of cotton floss. The design sizes and amounts of thread given are approximate.

Orange-and-black coaster

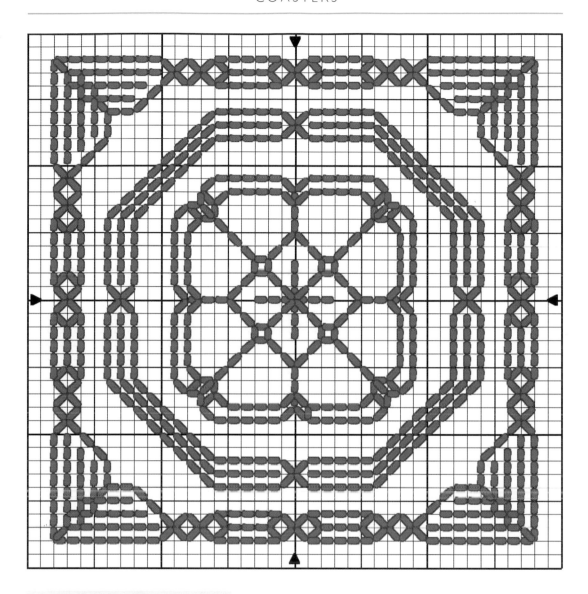

Design size
6.25 × 6.25cm (2½ × 2½in)

Stitch count
36 × 36

Fabric
Zweigart Aida, 14 count, black
10 × 10cm (4 × 4in)

Threads required

		Anchor	DMC	Madeira	Amount
	Orange, dark	332	608/946	0206/0207	1.5m (5ft)

Simple black coaster

☒☒ *Skill level* Intermediate

☒☒ *Average completion time* Two to three days

52

Design size
7.5 × 7.5cm (2⅞ × 2⅞in)

Stitch count
40 × 40

Fabric
Zweigart Aida, 14 count, ivory
10 × 10cm (4 × 4in)

Threads required

		Anchor	DMC	Madeira	Amount
■	Black	403	310	Black	2m 10cm (6ft 9in)

Celtic flower coaster

☒ *Skill level* Beginner

☒☒ *Average completion time* Two days

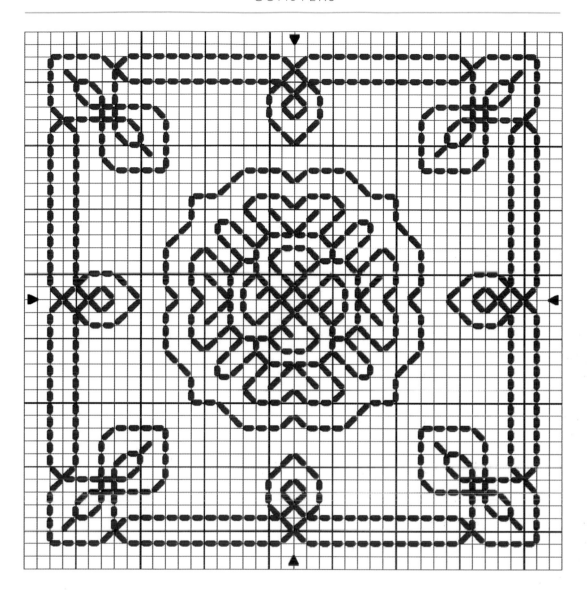

Design size
7 × 7cm (2¾ × 2¾in)

Stitch count
38 × 38

Fabric
Zweigart Aida,
14 count, cream
10 × 10cm (4 × 4in)

Threads required

		Anchor	DMC	Madeira	Amount
■	Cornflower blue, very dark	178	791	0904	1m 20cm (4ft)

Brown leaf coaster

☒☒☒ *Skill level* Experienced
☒☒☒ *Average completion time* Three days

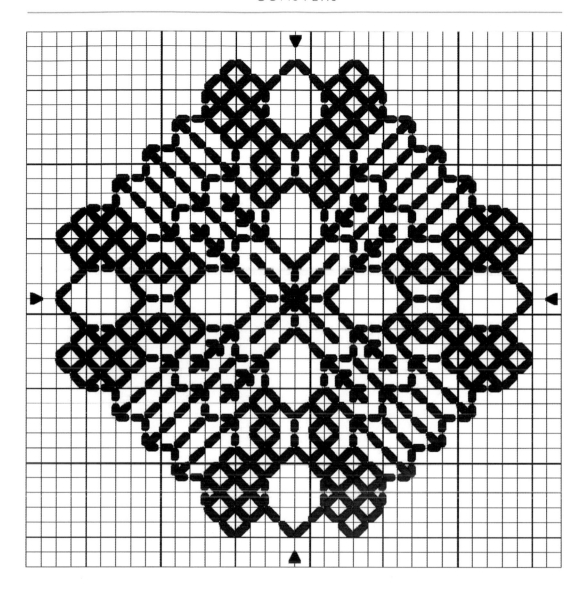

Design size
5.75 × 5.75cm (2¼ × 2¼in)

Stitch count
32 × 32

Fabric
Zweigart Aida, 14 count, cream
10 × 10cm (4 × 4in)

Threads required

		Anchor	DMC	Madeira	Amount
■	Black-brown, very dark	382	3371	2004	1m 20cm (4ft)

Spider-web coaster

☒☒☒ *Skill level* Experienced
☒☒☒ *Average completion time* Three days

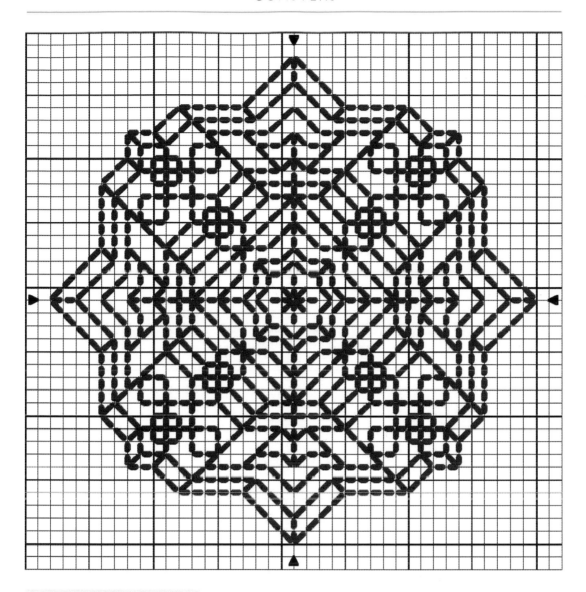

Design size
7 × 7cm (2¾ × 2¾in)

Stitch count
38 × 38

Fabric
Zweigart Aida, 14 count,
pearl grey
10 × 10cm (4 × 4in)

Threads required

		Anchor	DMC	Madeira	Amount
■	Mauve ultra, very dark	1029	915	0705	1m 60cm (5ft 2in)

Making up coasters

If your work needs washing, follow the instructions given in Chapter 1 (see p 17). If not, just follow the instructions for pressing (see p 17).

Fig 4.1
A coaster pack should contain a coaster blank, a card insert and a back plate

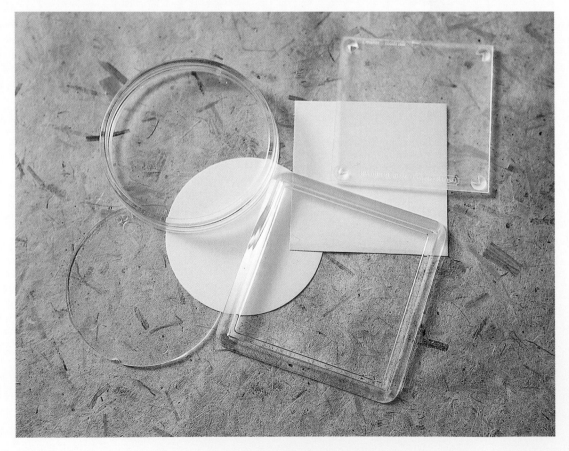

Place your work face down on a clean towel and place the interfacing on top of it, with the slightly shiny side down, matching the corners as best you can. Fix in place by dabbing the whole surface with a medium-hot iron: if you drag the iron, you may end up with the creases fused into the layers. When you are happy that the two layers are fully fused, switch off the iron and leave it to cool.

Transfer your work to a firm surface that is clean and dry. Undo the coaster pack and spread out its contents; you should have a coaster blank, a card insert and a back plate. Using the clear plastic back plate as a pattern (this is fractionally bigger than the size of the finished piece), place it on the reverse side of your work, centre the design under it, and trace around it. Cut around your outline using embroidery scissors to ensure a sharp, crisp cut. Try your work in the recess of the coaster blank to see if it fits neatly. If it bulges, remove it and trim back a little more. Be careful not to cut too much off or gaps will show around the edge, which will spoil the finished effect.

When you are happy with the fit, place the coaster blank face down and insert your finished design (also face down) into the recess. Place the card insert on top and, finally, lay the back plate on the card. Some back plates have a right and a wrong side; if there is any moulded writing, feet or marks on the plates, make sure these face the outside of the assembled layers or the raised areas may prevent you from fixing the back plate in place. Press down hard all around the edge of the plate until you are sure that it is fixed under the lugs or rim that will hold it in place.

Once fully assembled your coaster is ready to use, but please remember that it is not watertight so don't immerse it in water to wash it, simply wipe over the surface with a clean, damp cloth.

5 | Scented sachets

For me, living in England, nothing evokes pleasant memories of long (not very often), hot (sometimes) summers like the smell of lavender. As children, we used leftover scraps of material to make little lavender sachets which we put in our clothes drawers and wardrobes. My mother grew lavender in her garden, as did many of our neighbours, and in the evening the warm air was heavy with its scent. I have a profusion of lavender bushes in my own garden, partly for the luxury of being able to harvest the flowers but also because I just can't imagine having a garden without it. Everyone has their own preferences from the wide variety of scented flowers and plants that grow around the world. Fill these sachets with your favourites and bring your happiest memories alive again.

All the projects in this chapter have been stitched using six-stranded cotton floss; the tube sachets use only one strand but the square sachets use two. The design sizes and amounts of thread given are approximate.

Peach tube sachet

⊠⊠⊠ *Skill level* Experienced
⊠⊠⊠ *Average completion time* Two to three days

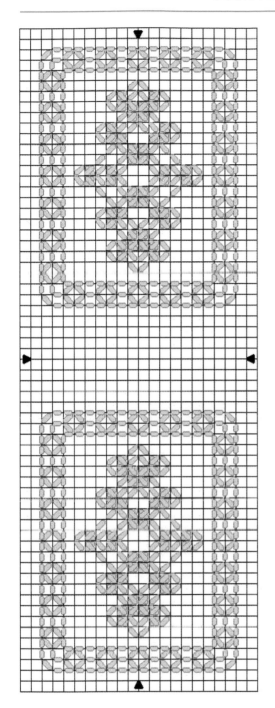

Design size
3 × 10cm (1¼ × 4in)

Stitch count
18 × 58

Fabric
Zweigart Aida band, 14 count, black
15 × 5cm (6 × 2in)

Threads required

		Anchor	DMC	Madeira	Amount
	Peach, very light	6	353	0304	1m 60cm (5ft 2in)

Hot pink tube sachet

☒☒ *Skill level* Intermediate
☒☒ *Average completion time* Two to three days

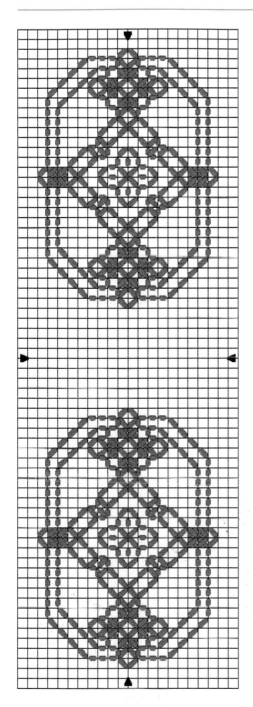

Design size
3 × 10.5cm (1¼ × 4¼in)

Stitch count
18 × 62

Fabric
Zweigart Aida band, 14 count, black
15 × 5cm (6 × 2in)

Threads required

		Anchor	DMC	Madeira	Amount
	Violet, light	97	No equiv.	No equiv.	1m 20cm (4ft)

Violet tube sachet

⊠⊠ *Skill level* Intermediate
⊠⊠⊠ *Average completion time* Two to three days

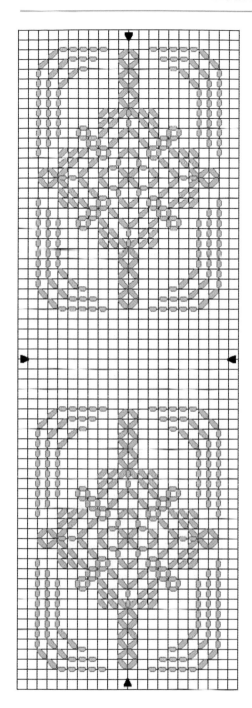

Design size
3 × 10.5cm (1¼ × 4¼in)

Stitch count
18 × 62

Fabric
Zweigart Aida band, 14 count, black
15 × 5 cm (6 × 2in)

Threads required

		Anchor	DMC	Madeira	Amount
	Mauve, very light	85	3609	0710	1m 10cm (4ft 8in)

Shades-of-summer square sachet

☒☒ *Skill level* Intermediate

☒☒☒ *Average completion time* Three to four days

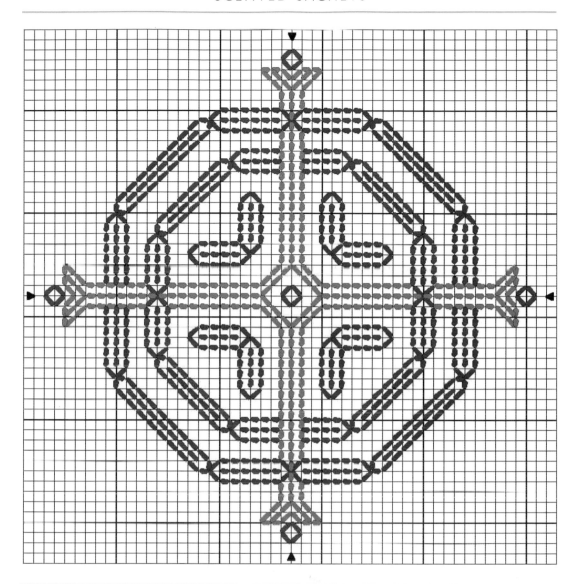

Design size
8 × 8cm (3¼ × 3¼in)

Stitch count
48 × 48

Fabric
Zweigart Aida, 14 count, ivory
11.5 × 11.5cm (4½ × 4½in)

Threads required

		Anchor	DMC	Madeira	Amount
	Lavender, very dark	112	No equiv.	No equiv.	65cm (2ft)
	Blue-purple, medium	122	No equiv.	No equiv.	50cm (1ft 8in)
	Violet, medium	99	55260	0713	45cm (1ft 5in)

Flowers square sachet

☒ *Skill level* Beginner

☒☒☒ *Average completion time* Three to four days

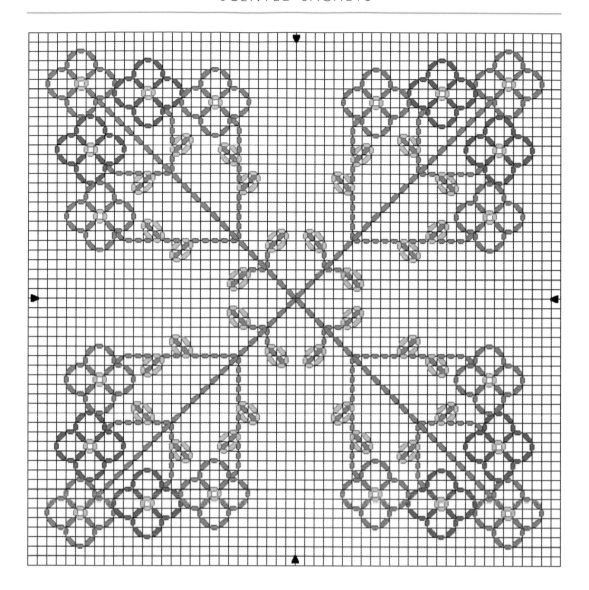

Design size
9.5 × 9.5cm (3¾ × 3¾in)

Stitch count
52 × 52

Fabric
Zweigart Aida, 14 count, black
12.5 × 12.5cm (5 × 5in)

Threads required

		Anchor	DMC	Madeira	Amount
	Fern green, light	859	523/3052	1509/1512	65cm (2ft)
	Peach, dark	329	608/946	0206/0207	50cm (1ft 8in)
	Orange, dark	332	608/946	0206/0207	40cm (1ft 4in)
	Sea-foam green, very light	875	503	1702	40cm (1ft 4in)
	Burnt orange, medium	302	743	0113	13cm (5in)

Making up scented sachets

TUBE SACHETS

Tools and materials
Thin braid or ribbon, 24cm (9in)
Double-edged, slotted lace, 13cm (5in)
Lavender or other dry pot-pourri
Fabric stiffener
Sharp sewing needle
Cotton floss in suitable colour
Embroidery scissors
Pins

If your work needs to be washed, follow the instructions given in Chapter 1 (see p 17). If not, just follow the instructions for pressing (see p 17).

Make sure you have the same number of holes after the design at each end. If you don't, cut the fabric down at the longer end, to match the shorter. Fold the Aida band in half lengthways, ensuring that the two halves of the design lie on top of each other correctly and that the scalloped edges align. Using two strands of cotton floss in the colour that you used to stitch the design, stitch up the edges along the set of holes closest to the scalloped edging; use running stitch, and stitch right to the top of the Aida. Paint a little fabric stiffener along the last row of blocks around the top edge of the sachet, and leave it to dry for about 1 hour. Fold the lace in half and pin this along the top edge of the tube, making sure that you cover the raw edge of the fabric sufficiently both inside and out. Overlap the ends of the lace at one side of the tube.

Stitch the lace into place with a thread to match its main colour; use tiny running stitches so that they are concealed in the lace, and turn the raw end of the lace under a little before stitching it in place. Next, take your braid or ribbon and either thread it through the slots in the lace or, as I have, through the tunnel made by the fold of the lace, bringing it in and out at the set of holes nearest one of the side seams.

If you are using ribbon, you can either tie a knot at the end of the length now, fill the sachet with your chosen pot-pourri, then pull it tight, or you can fill the sachet first, then pull the ribbon tight and tie a little bow to keep it closed.

If you are using braid, do not pull it tight; bind the two ends approximately 5mm (¼in) away from the side seam, using a complementary or contrasting colour in six-stranded cotton floss (not separated), and form a tassel following the instructions in Chapter 3 (see p 45). Fill the tube with your chosen pot-pourri and pull the braid tight to close the sachet. The braid should be thick enough to prevent the top opening by itself, but if it does open, tie a knot to stop it.

You can use the loop formed by the braid or ribbon to hang your sachets on a coat hanger or a hook in the wall. However you choose to use or display them, the beauty of these little tubes is that they can be refilled over and over again, so they will give you many years' service.

overlapping end of lace

scalloped edge of fabric

Fig 5.1 Pinning the folded lace along the top edge of the tube

SQUARE SACHETS

Tools and materials

Both designs
Aida in same colour as used for front
Lavender or other suitable dry pot-pourri
Sewing thread in suitable colour
Sharp sewing needle
Fabric stiffener
Pins

Shades-of-summer sachet
Thin braid × 2 lengths, 45cm (18in) long or ribbon × 2 lengths,
1.25 × 45cm (½ × 18in)
Pre-gathered lace, 1.75 × 47.5cm (¾ × 19in)

Flowers sachet
Chunky braid × 8 lengths, 20cm (8in) long or ribbon × 8 lengths,
1.25 × 20cm (½ × 8in)

For both designs, count the number of unstitched holes around the design area and trim the fabric back where necessary, so that all four sides are even. Cut your backing Aida to the same size. Paint a little fabric stiffener along the row of blocks nearest the raw edge on all sides of both pieces of fabric (design and backing) and leave to dry for about 1 hour.

Shades-of-summer sachet

Pin one length of braid along each side of both pieces of Aida. Leave no overhang at the corners but ensure that you fold the raw ends of the braid into the sachet (see Fig 5.2); this will hide them, and keep the braid from unravelling. Stitch the braid in place, using running stitch and a suitably coloured thread. Place the two Aida pieces together, with the design facing out, and position the lace between the outer edges of the braid along each side. Pin and then stitch in place around three sides (see Fig 5.3), fill the sachet with your chosen pot-pourri, then stitch up the final side, taking care to position the lace correctly. If your lace has a thin line of fabric stitched over the gathered edge, make sure this is concealed by the braid. If you want to renew the pot-pourri at a later date, carefully unpick the stitching along one edge of the braid, empty out the old pot-pourri, refill, then stitch up again. Make sure you fasten off any loose ends of the old stitching.

Flowers sachet

Pin a length of braid along each side of both pieces of Aida, leaving an extra 3.75cm (1½in) overhanging at each end, and ensuring that you have covered the last two blocks along the edge of the fabric. Using running stitch and a suitably coloured thread, stitch the braid in place. Next, align your two Aida pieces, with the design facing out, then pin the outer edges of the braid strips along three sides together. Use a tiny running stitch to close these three sides, then fill the sachet with your chosen pot-pourri and stitch up the final side of the braid. Form the tassels following the instructions given in Chapter 3 (see p 45) and your sachet will be ready for display.

If you want to renew the pot-pourri at a later date, carefully unpick the stitching along one edge of the braid, shake out the old pot-pourri, refill, then stitch up the braid again; make sure you fasten off any loose ends of the old stitching too.

raw ends of braid folded in

front of design

opening for pot-pourri

lace to decorate fourth side of sachet

Fig 5.2
(Far left) Folding the raw ends of the braid into the sachet

Fig 5.3
(Left) Fill your sachet before stitching up the final side

6 | Pincushions

Obviously, as stitchers, we use a lot of pins and needles. The little boxes or folders they come in are often so small, they make separating a single pin or needle a difficult task indeed. I have lost count of the number of times I've tipped up a whole box of pins as I tried to pick one out. So, I have included a couple of designs for pincushions that I hope you will find useful.

Both of these projects use two strands of cotton floss. The design sizes and amounts of thread given are approximate.

Flower pincushion

☒ *Skill level* Beginner

☒☒ *Average completion time* Two days

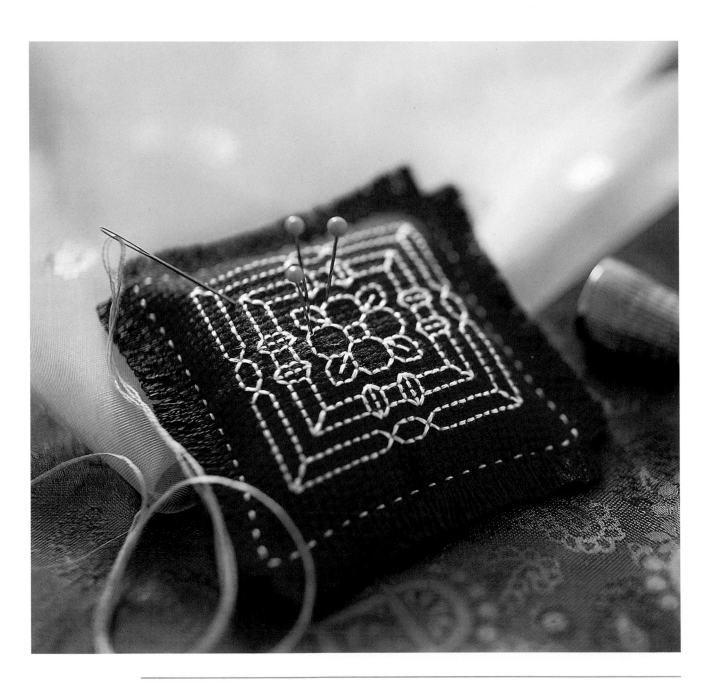

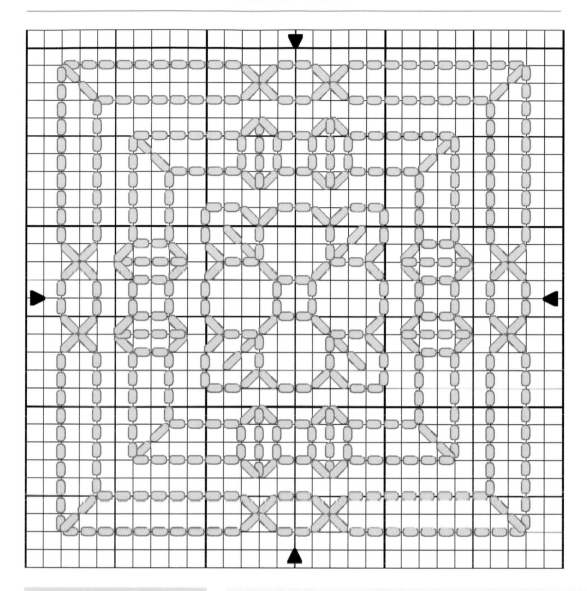

Design size
5 × 5cm (2 × 2in)

Stitch count
26 × 26

Fabric
Zweigart Aida,
14 count, dark red
7.5 × 7.5cm (3 × 3in)

Threads required

		Anchor	DMC	Madeira	Amount
	Peach, very light	6	353	0304	80cm (2ft 7in)

Brick pincushion

☒☒☒ *Skill level* Experienced
☒☒☒ *Average completion time* Three days

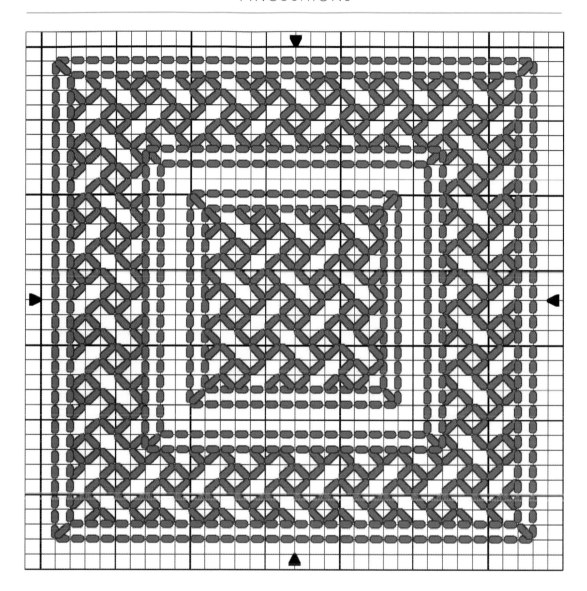

Design size
5.75 × 5.75cm (2¼ × 2¼in)

Stitch count
32 × 32

Fabric
Zweigart Aida, 14 count, black
8.75 × 8.75cm (3½ × 3½in)

Threads required

	Anchor	DMC	Madeira	Amount
Mauve	87	3607	No equiv.	1m 80cm (6ft)

Making up pincushions

Tools and materials
Aida in same colour as used for front
Flame-retardant polyester toy filling
Cotton floss in suitable colour
Sharp sewing needle
Embroidery scissors
Fabric stiffener
Pins

If your work needs to be washed, follow the instructions given in Chapter 1 (see p 17). If not, just follow the instructions for pressing (see p 17).

Ensure that you have the same number of holes remaining on all four sides of your design, then cut the backing Aida to the same size. Lay one Aida piece on top of the other, with the design facing out. Using the same colour and number of strands of floss as you used to stitch the design, join the two pieces together with a neat row of running stitches, a minimum of two to three blocks away from the edge of the design, along three sides. Stuff the cushion to the required firmness with the toy filling, then stitch up the final side.

Paint the Aida, between the edge of the fabric and the running stitches, with fabric stiffener and, *before* it dries, carefully remove the horizontal threads one at a time. Start at the edge of the fabric and work inwards until you reach the row of holes one block away from your running stitch seam on both pieces of Aida.

As the fabric stiffener dries, it will harden the fringe and prevent it from fraying any further. To add a more decorative touch, you could always trim the cushion with braid and add tassels as I did for the square scented sachets in Chapter 5 (see pp 76 and 77).

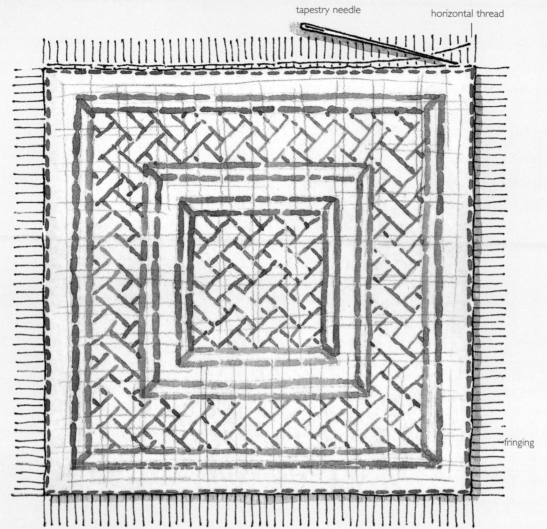

tapestry needle

horizontal thread

Fig 6.1
Use a tapestry needle to loosen the horizontal threads; this will make it easier to remove them

fringing

7 | Cards

Nothing shows how much you care more than a card made especially for the person concerned. I have put together this group of three celebration cards, but don't let my choice of greetings put you off making them. It would be quite easy to add alternative greetings for any special occasion, so why not give it a try?

All the projects in this chapter use two strands of cotton floss; the Christmas card also uses four strands of metallic stranded thread. The design sizes and amounts of thread given for the cards are approximate.

Mother's Day card

☒☒ *Skill level* Intermediate
☒☒ *Average completion time* Two to three days

Design size
8 × 8cm (3¼ × 3¼in)

Stitch count
46 × 46

Fabric
Zweigart Aida, 14 count, ivory
12.5 × 12.5cm (5 × 5in)

Card
Three-fold with 8.5cm (3¼in)
circular aperture

Threads required

		Anchor	DMC	Madeira	Amount
	Mauve, medium	87	3067	No equiv.	25cm (10in)
	Lavender, medium	109	209	0803	23cm (9in)
	Sky blue, light	130	809	0909	18cm (7in)
	Sky blue, medium	131	798	0911	33cm (13in)
	Forest green, medium	256	704/906	1308/1411	15cm (6in)
	Forest green, very dark	258	904	1413	13cm (5in)

Father's Day card

☒☒ *Skill level* Intermediate
☒☒ *Average completion time* Two days

90

Design size
5 × 6.75cm (2 × 2¾in)

Stitch count
28 × 38

Fabric
Zweigart Aida, 14 count, white
10 × 12.5cm (4 × 5in)

Card
Three-fold with
5.5 × 7.5cm (2¼ × 3in)
rectangular aperture

Threads required

		Anchor	DMC	Madeira	Amount
	Sky blue, light	130	809	0909	35cm (1ft 2in)
	Sky blue, medium	131	798	0911	28cm (11in)
	Cornflower blue, very dark	178	791	0904	50cm (1ft 8in)

Christmas card

☒☒ *Skill level* Intermediate
☒☒ *Average completion time* Two to three days

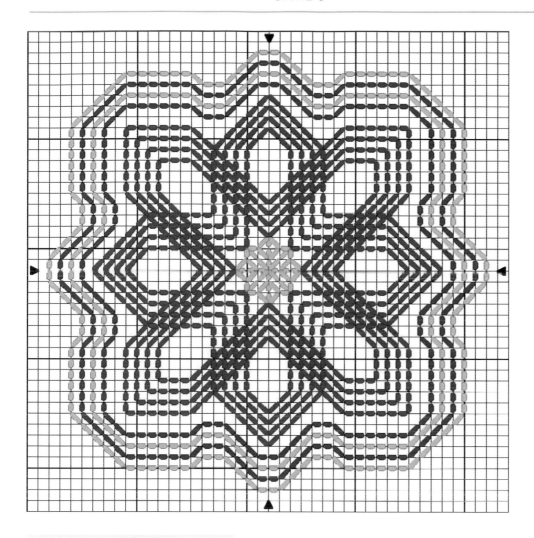

Design size
6 × 6cm (2¼ × 2¼in)

Stitch count
40 × 40

Fabric
Zweigart Aida, 14 count, black
12.5 × 12.5cm (5 × 5in)

Card
Three-fold with 8.5cm (3¼in)
circular aperture

Threads required

		Anchor	DMC	Madeira	Amount
	Metallic gold	303	5284	No equiv.	98cm (3ft 3in)
	Christmas red, light	923	699/909	1303/13021	40cm (1ft 4in)
	Christmas green, very dark	46	666	0210	50cm (1ft 8in)

Making up cards

Tools and materials
Three-fold card, aperture size as stated for design
Double-sided adhesive tape
Felt, same colour as Aida, same size as aperture of card
Pencil or tailor's chalk

If your work needs to be washed, follow the instructions given in Chapter 1 (see p 17). If not, just follow the instructions for pressing (see p 17).

Open out your card so that the aperture is in the middle, cut suitable lengths of the adhesive tape and arrange these around the edge of the aperture and along the top, bottom and both sides of this part of the card. Be careful not to let the tape extend beyond the edge of the aperture or the area just to the left of the fold; if it does, the tape will show when the card is opened, and the right-hand side of the card may stick to it.

Before you go any further, it is vitally important to check that you have the card the right way up as some cards have a deeper section below the aperture than above it. When the card is made up, you should have the fold on the left-hand side and the opening on the right-hand side. Checking this now will save a lot of time and heartache; even if you think you've got it right, it is always best to check again, just to be on the safe side.

Fig 7.1
Sticking double-sided tape around the aperture

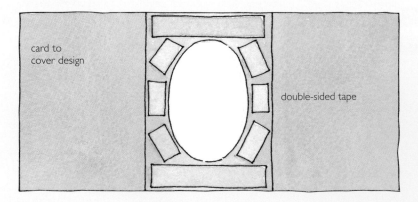

card to cover design

double-sided tape

Now lay your work face down, place the card over it and centre your design in the aperture as best you can. Using a pencil or tailor's chalk, make a small mark on the fabric at the top, bottom and both sides of the aperture, then remove the card. These marks will help you check the positioning of the design.

Fold the card up as you would to finish, and carefully turn it over so that the design is facing you. Check that the design is still in the right position. If you are not happy with this, now is the time to fix it: you will not be able to make any adjustments once the card has been fully assembled. A good way to check is to count the number of holes from each side of the design to the edge of the aperture – they should match.

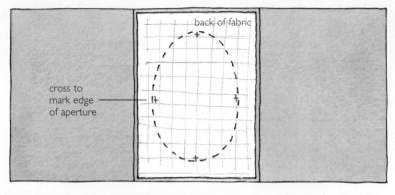

Fig 7.2
Marking off the edges of the aperture

Once you are happy with the positioning, open out the card again, trying to avoid the design slipping. Holding the Aida in place with one hand, carefully peel the backing from the lengths of tape you have placed around the aperture and press the fabric down onto this. Working from the centre, smooth the fabric outwards to ensure that there are no creases or wrinkles. If the fabric bulges a little as you do this, lift the edge off the tape so that you can smooth it away, then press it firmly into place again.

Place the felt on the reverse side of the design, in line with the aperture. Now remove the backing from the tape that you placed along the top, bottom and sides of the card and, again, press down and smooth the card until it is fixed firmly in place. This time, work from the folded edge of the card, smoothing towards the top and bottom edges so it doesn't twist and crease; you will not be able to lift the card off the tape without tearing it, and any twists or creases will spoil its appearance and the way it lies when folded.

Finally, add your greetings to the inside of the card, and it is ready to send.

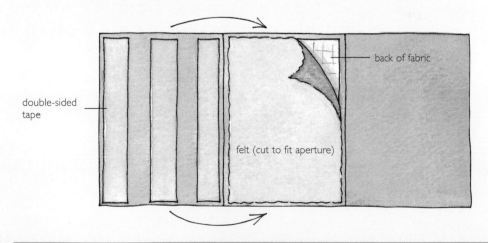

Fig 7.3
Folding the left-hand side of the card over the felt-backed design

95

8 | Celtic chessboard

When considering what would make a good main project for this book I looked at various options, most of which I discarded on the basis that they had already been used in other books: I was looking to create something a little more unusual. I wanted to present projects that were a little out of the ordinary to get you trying something different, and I wanted to develop some new ideas I had for blackwork (a form of stitching much favoured by the Tudors), but in a more modern way. It was in following these thoughts that I came up with the chessboard. I have included instructions for finishing this project as a framed design or as a wall hanging. If you don't play chess and have no suitable recipients for this project, try the cushion design that has been adapted from this (see Chapter 9, p 122).

This project has been stitched using two strands of cotton floss. The design sizes and amounts of thread given are approximate.

Celtic
chessboard

☒☒☒ *Skill level* Experienced

☒☒☒☒ *Average completion time*
Four to six weeks

Design size
28.25 × 38.25cm (11⅝ × 15¼in)

Stitch count
162 × 214

Fabric
Zweigart Aida, 14 count, ivory
40 × 50cm (16 × 20in)

Threads required

		Anchor	DMC	Madeira	Amount
⬛	Black	403	310	Black	30m 48cm (101ft 7in)

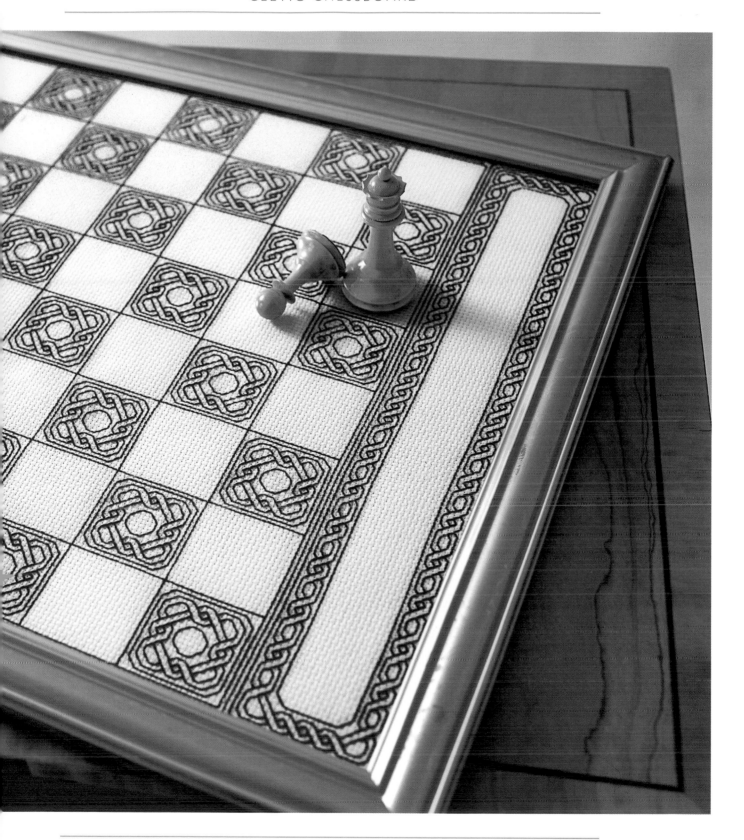

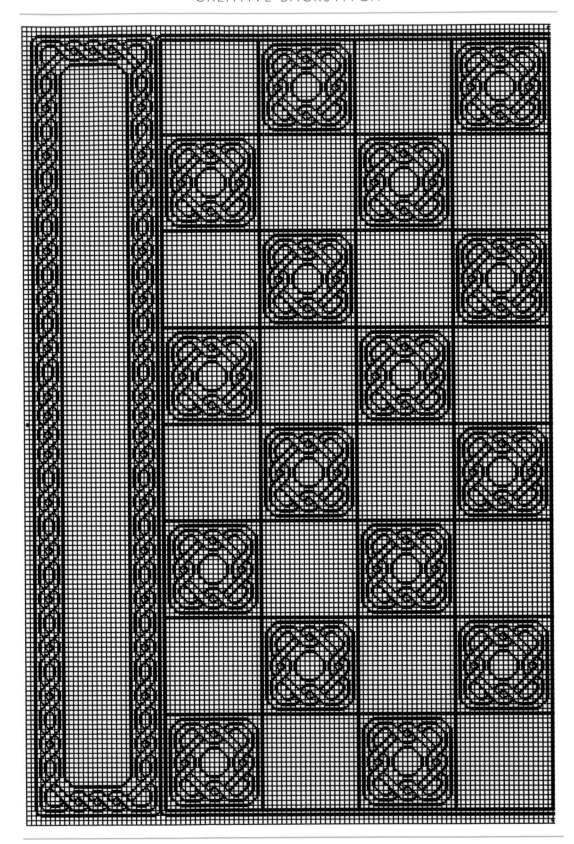

Making up the chessboard design

Tools and materials
Acid-free mount board, 27.5 × 37.5cm (11 × 15in)
Picture or photo frame, 30 × 40cm (12 × 16in)
Lightweight polyester wadding,
26.25 × 36.25cm (10½ × 14½in)
Strong thread, suitable for lacing the fabric
Plastic-coated, self-adhesive tape
Methylated spirit
Sharp sewing needle
Pins

This design was made to fit a standard photo frame in order to help keep costs down by avoiding the necessity for professional framing. Of course, if you prefer to have your work professionally framed, there is no reason not to do so.

Your work will probably need to be washed, as you will have spent quite some time working on it, so follow the instructions for washing and pressing given in Chapter 1 (see p 17).

FRAMED CHESSBOARD

Place your acid-free mount board on a clean, firm surface and lay your wadding on top, ensuring that it doesn't overhang the edges of the board, as the extra thickness of the wadding would make it too big for the frame. Lay your chessboard design on the wadding, face up. Centre the design, then check that the wadding hasn't moved; if it has, realign all the layers before proceeding any further. Push a pin into the edge of the mount board at each of the four corners to hold the design in place.

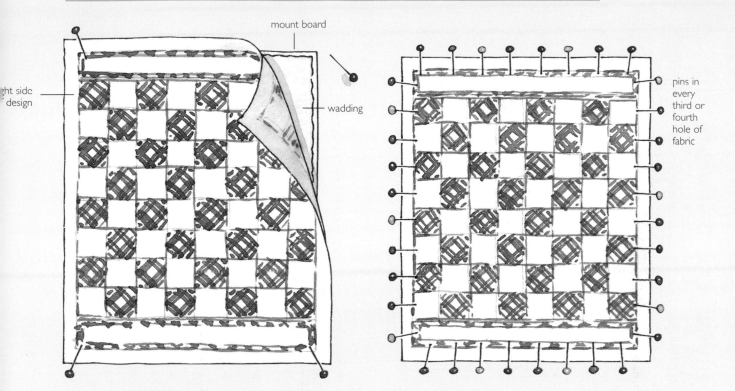

right side of design — mount board — wadding — pins in every third or fourth hole of fabric

Now, using the holes in the Aida as your guide to achieve a straight line, push pins into the edge of the mount board, at intervals of three or four holes, all the way along the top of the board. Remove the two pins at the bottom corners and pull the fabric gently over the bottom edge to stretch it slightly. Be careful not to pull the fabric so much that the mount board bends or you will distort your work. Pin the fabric in place in the same manner as for the top edge.

Fig 8.1
(Above left) Pinning the design on the mount board

Fig 8.2
(Above right) Fixing the design firmly in place

Repeat this procedure for the sides, then check that all the lines on the design are still straight; if they are not, simply re-pin the offending side to reduce the tension slightly. Now turn you work over so that it is ready to lace, taking care not to disturb any pins.

Thread your sharp needle with the strong thread. Tie a good-sized knot in the end and, using an over and under pattern, start lacing your work from top to bottom (see Fig 8.3, overleaf), working from one side towards the middle. When you reach the middle, remove the thread from your needle, but do not fasten it off at this point. Thread your needle with a new length and start again, this time working from the other side towards the middle. Now go back to the first side and take up the slack from the thread, one lacing at a time. Do the same on the other side, then knot the two ends together in the middle.

end of lacing from one side   back of chessboard

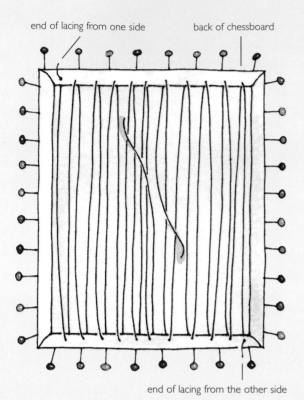

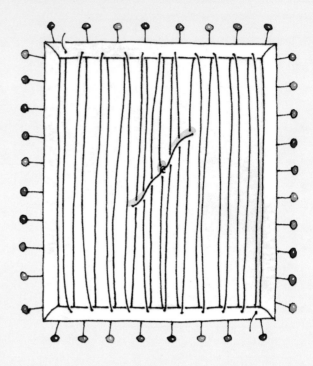

end of lacing from the other side

Fig 8.3
(Above left) Lacing the chessboard from top to bottom; work from one side to the middle, then start again at the other

Fig 8.4
(Above right) Gently pull the threads to take up any slack before tying the two ends together

Fig 8.5
(Right) Lacing up the sides of the chessboard

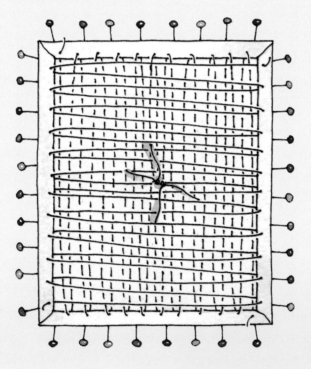

Repeat this whole lacing process for the sides, taking up the slack and tying both ends in the middle as before (see Fig 8.5).

Fold in the corners, making them as flat as possible, and stitch in place. You can now remove all the pins from each side.

Clean the inside of the glass – methylated spirit is good for this, but make sure the glass is completely dry before placing your work on it or the alcohol will stain and weaken the fabric. Check again that the design has not been distorted in any way, then lay it face down in the frame. Place the backboard in the frame on top of your work and, using the clips provided, secure in place. Cut suitable lengths of the plastic-coated tape and use these to seal the gap between the backboard and the edge of the frame. Your chessboard is now ready for use – and it doubles as an interesting picture.

Corners

Your corners may not form a neat, symmetrical shape, especially if you have slightly more fabric on one side, but don't worry about this; all that matters is that they are flat.

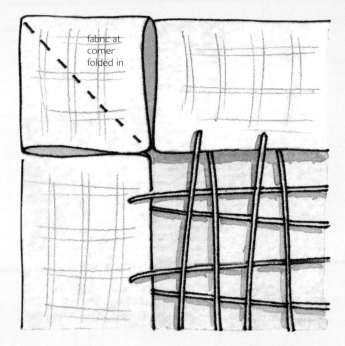

Fig 8.6 Fold in the corners as though wrapping a present

WALL HANGING

Tools and materials
Lightweight polyester wadding, 37.55 × 47.5cm (15 × 19in)
Backing fabric, same size as Aida
Bell-pull rods × 2, 37.5cm (15in) wide
Braid, approx. 55cm (22in) long
Sewing machine or sharp sewing needle
Sewing thread in suitable colour
Cotton floss in suitable colour
Tapestry needle
Damp cloth
Iron
Pins

Wash and press your backing material to avoid it shrinking and distorting your work at a later date. Lay your design face up on a clean, firm surface, then lay the backing material face down on top of this and smooth out any creases or wrinkles. Pin the pieces together along each side but not the top and bottom, then stitch these seams, by machine or by hand, leaving a 12mm (½in) allowance on both sides. Turn this

Fig 8.7 Securing
the bell-pull rods

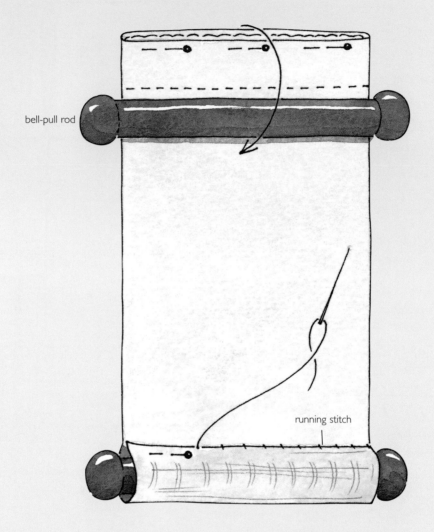

bell-pull rod

running stitch

'tube' inside out so that you have the right side of the design facing you, and push out the fabric at the sides to avoid any bunching inside the seams. Place a slightly damp cloth over the seams and press them flat with a medium-hot iron.

Feed the polyester wadding between the fabric layers, smoothing out any bulges. Make sure the wadding goes right up to the edges of the side seams and that there is the same amount of spare fabric beyond it at the top and bottom edges. From the raw edge, fold in approximately 5mm (¼in) of both the Aida and the backing fabric at the top and bottom of the design and pin in place. Now turn the wall hanging over so that you have the backing facing you. Lay one bell-pull rod across the width of the fabric at the top and do the same with the other at the bottom.

Fold the fabric over each rod to form a narrow tunnel and, using the pins you already have in the top and bottom edges, pin in place. To secure the rods, hand stitch a line of running stitches across the width of the fabric. You should now have a scroll effect, with your bell-pull rods at the top and bottom of the wall hanging and the design in between.

Loop your braid around each end of the top rod, with the raw ends of the braid to the back (see Fig 8.8). Cut a 15–20cm (6–8in) length of suitably coloured cotton floss (not separated) and wind one end tightly around the braid, ensuring that the raw end is covered (see Fig 8.8). Thread the other end of the floss through a tapestry needle, pass this under the floss binding, on the reverse side of your work, and pull the thread tight. Fasten off by passing the needle under and over the binding several times, until you are sure that the thread won't work loose. Cut off any excess as close to the binding as possible. Repeat this process at the other end of the bell-pull rod. Your chessboard is now ready, and when not in use, can form an interesting decoration for your home.

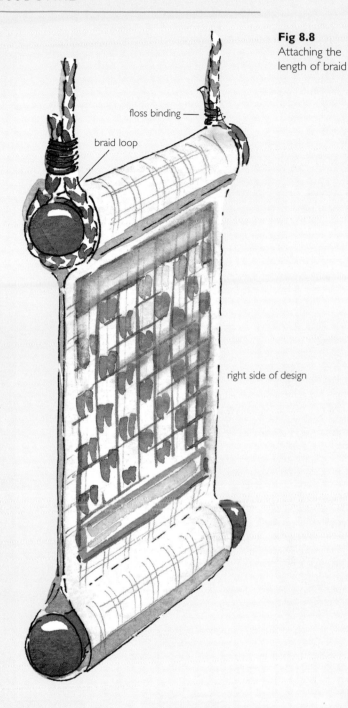

Fig 8.8
Attaching the length of braid

floss binding —

braid loop

right side of design

Part Three
Adaptations

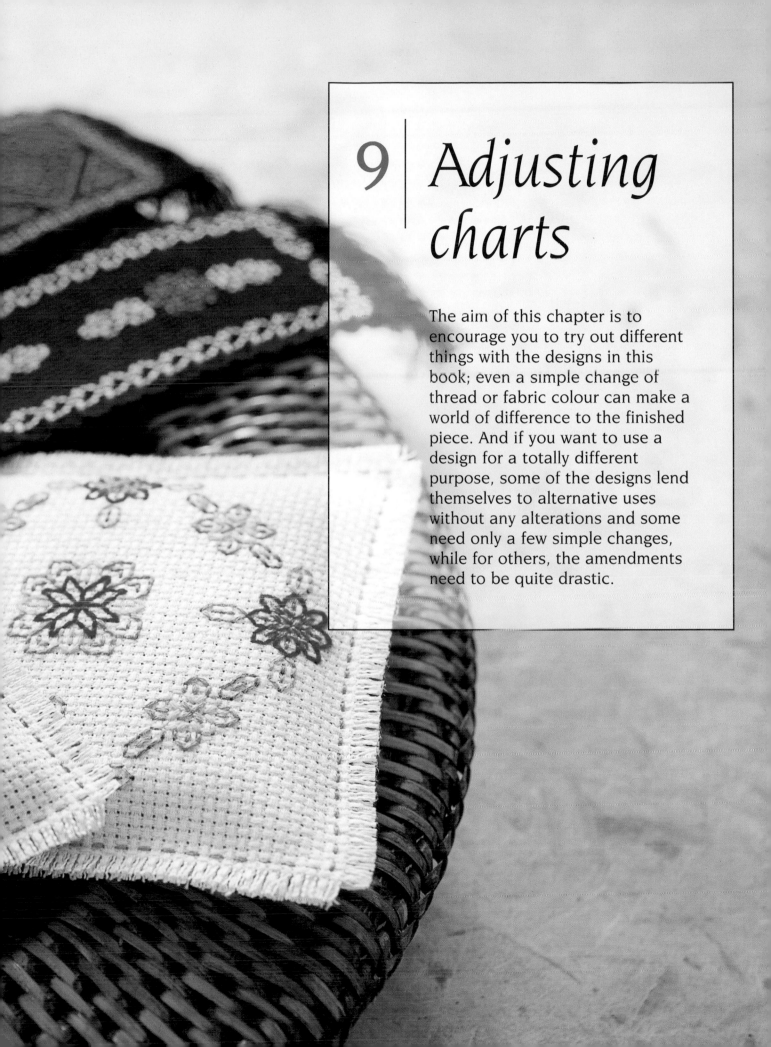

9 | Adjusting charts

The aim of this chapter is to encourage you to try out different things with the designs in this book; even a simple change of thread or fabric colour can make a world of difference to the finished piece. And if you want to use a design for a totally different purpose, some of the designs lend themselves to alternative uses without any alterations and some need only a few simple changes, while for others, the amendments need to be quite drastic.

I have included some adaptations here to show you how easy it is, and to give you a greater choice of projects to make, especially if you need something in a hurry, but I really hope you will try altering some of them yourself

A good place to start is with the bookmark designs. Try adapting them to make tube sachets; all you need to do is decide where to break the pattern to give you two identical sides. Or how about cutting the two diamond shapes out of the Father's Day card border to make it square; this could then be used to decorate a coaster, a pincushion or a square sachet.

Once you start to experiment, the possibilities are endless – I must warn you that the hobby can become addictive. Don't stop at adapting my designs; try out different ideas yourself. Look around and you will soon find that you see suitable patterns in so many of the ordinary, everyday things you once took for granted. Before long you will find yourself coming up with totally new designs.

All the projects in this chapter have been stitched using two strands of cotton floss. The design sizes and amounts of thread given are approximate.

Flowers needle case

☒ *Skill level* Beginner
☒☒ *Average completion time* Two days

Having made a pincushion, it would be nice to have a matching needle case. The pincushion designs are very easy to adapt – it is just a case of repeating the design to make it into a rectangle instead of a square. Try this idea on other square designs to see the effect.

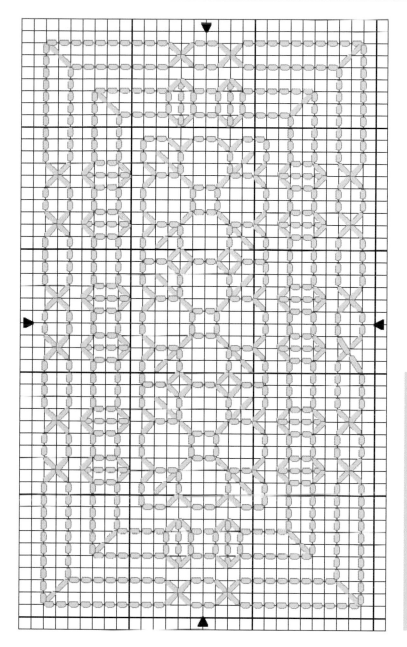

Design size
5 × 8cm
(1⁷⁄₈ × 3¹⁄₄in)

Stitch count
26 × 16

Fabric
Zweigart Aida,
14 count, dark red
6 × 25cm
(2¹⁄₂ × 5¹⁄₂in)

Threads required

		Anchor	DMC	Madeira	Amount
	Peach, very light	6	353	0304	1m 38cm (4ft 7in)

Brick needle case

☒☒☒ *Skill level* Experienced
☒☒☒ *Average completion time* Two to three days

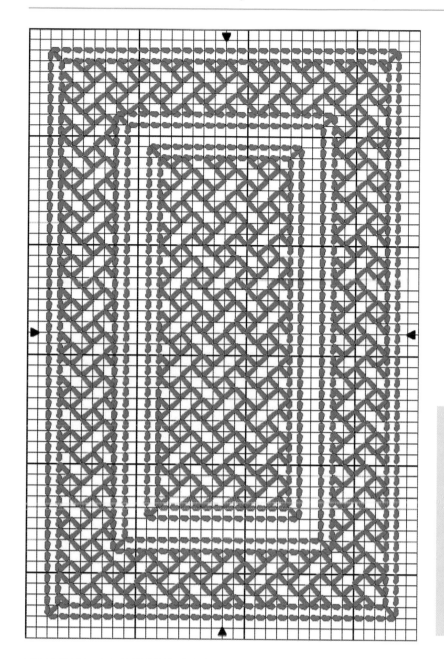

Design size
6 × 9.5cm (2¼ × 3¾in)

Stitch count
32 × 52

Fabric
Zweigart Aida,
14 count, black
15 × 11.25cm (6 × 4⁷⁄₁₆in)

Threads required

		Anchor	DMC	Madeira	Amount
▨	Mauve	87	3607	No equiv.	2m 78cm (9ft 3in)

Floral square sachet

☒☒ *Skill level* Intermediate
☒☒☒ *Average completion time* Three to four days

How about a scented sachet adapted from the Mother's Day card? With a little rearranging of the flowers and leaves, it can be made more diamond-like in shape; add a central flower to replace the wording and you have a design that is perfect for a scented sachet. Rotate the design to form a square, work on 18-count fabric in place of 14-count, and you can make a coaster.

Design size
8 × 8cm (3¼ × 3¼in)

Stitch count
46 × 46

Fabric
Zweigart Aida,
14 count, ivory
10 × 10cm (4 × 4in)

Alternative fabric
Zweigart Aida,
14 count, cream for
a warmer feel or black
for a more
dramatic effect

	Threads required	Anchor	DMC	Madeira	Amount
	Mauve	87	3067	No equiv.	25cm (10in)
	Lavender	109	209	0803	33cm (1ft 1in)
	Sky blue, light	130	809	0909	25cm (10in)
	Sky blue, medium	131	798	0911	20cm (8in)
	Forest green, medium	256	704/906	1308/1411	18cm (7in)
	Forest green, very dark	258	904	1413	15cm (6in)

	Alternative threads	Anchor	DMC	Madeira
	Peach, dark	10	351	0214
	Peach, very dark	13	349/817	211/212
	Burnt orange, very dark	304	741	0201
	Lemon, very dark	291	798	0911
	Forest green, medium	256	704/906	1308/1411
	Forest green, very dark	258	904	1413

Flower bookmark

☒☒ *Skill level* Intermediate
☒☒ *Average completion time* **Two days**

Take the central flower from the design for the flower pincushion, increase the height by one stitch and reduce the width by one stitch. You now have a slightly different flower to work with. This time work a border from straight lines joined at appropriate places and you will have a totally different look.

Design size
4.75 × 20.5cm (1⅞ × 8in)

Stitch count
27 × 122

Fabric
Zweigart Aida, 14 count, black
6.25 × 28cm (2½ × 11in)

Threads required

		Anchor	DMC	Madeira	Amount
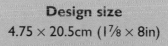	Orange-red	335	606	0209	3m 98cm (13ft 3in)

Chessboard cushion

⊠⊠⊠ *Skill level* Experienced
⊠⊠⊠ *Average completion time* Eight to ten weeks

I designed the chessboard in Chapter 8 as a result of family influences (my daughter is a keen player). However, after a little more thought (and some heavy hints from other family members), I realized that not everyone would want a chessboard, so I designed this cushion as an alternative. I have also included instructions for making up the design as a table mat. The chart shows the top left corner of the design; rotate it and reverse the order of the individual squares accordingly for the remaining three quarters.

Design size
31.25 × 31.25cm (12⅜ × 12⅜in)

Stitch count
174 × 174

Fabric
Zweigart Aida, 14 count, cream
40 × 40cm (16 × 16in)

Threads required

		Anchor	DMC	Madeira	Amount
	Topaz, medium	308	782	2212	16m 85cm (56ft 2in)
	Black-brown, medium	380	838	1914	14m 23cm (46ft 8in)
	Topaz, very dark	310	434/780	2009/2214	6m 18cm (20ft 7in)

Making up the projects

Instructions for making up some of the projects in this chapter have been given in previous chapters (for the bookmark see Chapter 3, p 42; for the coaster, Chapter 4, p 60; and for the scented sachet, Chapter 5, p 74). Instructions for the needle cases, cushion and table mat are given below.

NEEDLE CASES

> **Tools and materials**
> Felt, same colour and same size as fabric for needle case
> Felt, different colour from first piece,
> 12mm (½in) smaller than needle case in width and length
> Iron-on bonding webbing in sheet
> form, same size as fabric for needle case
> Sewing thread in suitable colour
> Sharp sewing needle
> Embroidery scissors
> Towel
> Iron
> Pins

If your work needs to be washed, follow the instructions given in Chapter 1 (see p 17). If not, just follow the instructions for pressing (see p 17).

Fold a clean, dry towel and place this on your ironing board. Lay your work face down on top of this, then lay the iron-on bonding webbing on top of your work, making sure that it goes right up to the edges of the fabric all the way around but not beyond, or you will end up bonding your work to the towel. Now take the piece of felt that is the same size as your needle case and lay that on top of the bonding webbing. With your iron set to medium-hot, fuse the three layers by carefully dabbing the iron on the felt; don't drag it as this can cause the fabrics to pucker and crease, which would spoil your work. When you are sure that the three layers have properly fused, right up to the edges, switch off your iron and leave it to cool.

Using bonding sheets

Some bonding sheets require a slightly different technique; always refer to the manufacturer's instructions.

Transfer your work to a clean, firm surface and, using embroidery scissors, trim back the top, bottom and right-hand edges neatly so that you have the same number of holes around the edge of the design on these three sides as between the fold and the left-hand side of the design. Now fold your needle case in half lengthways to form a 'book'; the fold should be on the left-hand side when the design is facing you. Make sure the top and bottom corners of the front sit exactly on the top and bottom corners of the back or your needle case will end up with a slight twist.

Fold the remaining, slightly smaller piece of felt in half and place it inside the needle case to form two 'pages'. Open the needle case out and line up the folds of the 'cover' and 'pages', making sure that you have the same size gap between the edge of the needle case and the edge of the inner felt all around. Once you are happy with the layout, pin the felt to your needle case along the centre folds; don't twist the inner felt as you pin or you may stitch it in slightly out of line, which would spoil the finished look. Using the same colour thread as you used for the design, stitch a neat row of running stitches – one per block of the Aida – along the folds to secure the inner felt and form the spine of your needle case. Your needle case is now ready to use. The felt pages will keep your needles safe and help to prevent them from rusting if they are not in regular use.

CHESSBOARD CUSHION

Tools and materials
Chosen backing fabric, in colour to complement or contrast with design
Cushion insert, 35cm (14in), or flame-retardant polyester toy filling
Sewing machine or sharp sewing needle
Velcro, 35cm (14in)
Sewing thread in suitable colour
Braid (optional), 2m (6ft 8in)
Towel
Pins

Wash and press your work following the instructions in Chapter 1 (see p 17), then wash and press your backing fabric to ensure that it will not shrink or distort after you have made up your cushion. Cut it into a 40cm (16in) square to match your Aida piece.

I like to use Velcro to fasten this type of project as it has no sharp metal edges, as a zip does, to tear the fabric of your furniture. If you are using polyester filling rather than a cushion insert, you will need to stitch up your final seam rather than fastening it with Velcro; follow the instructions below, but ignore those steps involving Velcro.

Separate the two layers of Velcro and pin one layer along the raw edge of one side of the backing fabric. Pin the other layer to one side of the design fabric in the same way. Now stitch both pieces in place, making sure that you stitch over each end of the Velcro to prevent the ends from pulling out of the seams.

Lay your backing fabric face up on a clean, firm surface, then place your design face down on top of it, lining up the two Velcro strips and smoothing out any creases or wrinkles. Pin the fabric pieces together along the other three sides and then stitch up the seams, by machine or by hand, leaving a 12mm (½in) allowance all around and ensuring that you have stitched over both ends of the Velcro.

Turn your cushion cover inside out so that you now have the right side outside. The fabric does tend to bunch up at the corners, making them slightly rounded. To remedy this, put your fingers inside the cover and push the material out to form neatly squared corners.

If you are using braid, cut it into four 50cm (20in) lengths, then tie a piece of thread around each cut end to keep it from unravelling before you want it to. Pin a length of braid along each side so that it covers the line of the seam and has an overhang of 6.25cm (2½in) at each end; this will form your tassel.

Hand stitch the braid in place using suitably coloured sewing thread and an ordinary sharp needle. Stitch into the edge of the braid that is nearest the fabric or your stitches will show. To form the tassels, follow the instructions given in Chapter 2 (see p 45).

With the tassels made, slip your cushion insert into the cover and press the Velcro together to close it. If you are using polyester filling, simply stuff your cushion to the required firmness now, and stitch up the final seam. Your cushion is now ready to use. Remember, it is not advisable to machine-wash the cover; for the best care of your cushion cover, follow the washing instructions given in Chapter 1 (see p 17).

CHESSBOARD TABLE MAT

Tools and materials
Felt, 31.25 × 31.25cm (12$\frac{5}{16}$ × 12$\frac{5}{16}$in)
Iron-on bonding webbing, same size as felt
Embroidery scissors
Tapestry needle
Towel
Iron

Wash and press your work following the instructions given in Chapter 1 (see p 17), then trim the fabric as necessary to ensure that you have the same number of holes around each side of the design.

Place a folded, clean, dry towel on your ironing board and lay your work face down on top of this. Lay the bonding webbing on top of your work; make sure it goes right up to the edges of the design all the way around and no more than one block beyond it, or it will glue the threads of the Aida together and you won't be able to fringe it properly. Lay the felt on top of this, smooth out any creases or wrinkles, then check that the two top layers are still correctly aligned with the design before proceeding any further. If they have moved even a little, reposition them and smooth out any creases or wrinkles as before.

With your iron on a medium-hot setting, fuse the three layers, working from the centre outwards to ensure a smooth, even finish. Dab the iron on the fabric: if you drag it, the layers may fuse with creases in them. Once you are sure that all the layers are secure, switch off your iron and leave it to cool.

Transfer your work to a clean, firm surface. It is now time to make the fringe. To do this, remove each of the horizontal threads from the outer edges of the fabric until you are one block away from the design; the remaining vertical threads will form the fringe (see Fig 6.1, p 85). Don't try to remove too many threads at the same time as this will cause them to tangle and you will distort the fabric as you pull. The best method is to remove one or two threads at a time, easing them out gently with the point of your tapestry needle: this will enable you to smooth out any potential tangles as you go. Work on one side at a time.

Your table mat is now ready to use. To wash it, follow the instructions given in Chapter 1 (see p 17). To dry it, lay it out flat and face down on a folded towel, untangle and straighten the fringe, then iron dry on a medium-hot, dry setting, taking care not to distort the shape of the mat as you go.

About the author

When I was a little girl my grandmother used to come and visit, as most grandparents do. She normally came every other Sunday and she liked to take my sister and I to one side to teach us the basic skills of knitting, crochet and creative needlework. The crochet, I have to admit, I never quite got the hang of, but the rest of it I did manage to master quite well, and with pleasing results.

However, as I grew up and became more independent, I became interested in other things. I much preferred being outside with my friends; I didn't want to spend my free time cooped up indoors working on the little projects my grandmother set us in between her visits. Like most children, I didn't appreciate how much it all meant to her and I complained constantly to my mother that it was a waste of time. I hoped to get her to intervene and save me from what had, by now, become a chore. Her answer was simple and one I have found myself giving to my own children on more than one occasion; 'No knowledge is ever wasted. You never know when something you have learnt, even if it seemed totally irrelevant at the time, will come in useful.' There was no help for me there. At least, that's what I thought back then.

The years passed and I went to work, first with horses at the local riding school, then in farming, and later in my husband's business. Then, suddenly, like a bolt from the blue, I discovered I had Multiple Sclerosis. My lifestyle changed completely. I now live a somewhat restricted life; no horses, no going for long, energetic walks in the countryside, and no wildly adventurous holidays with the kids. But, over the years, I have learnt to accept the restraints my health has placed on me and I have rediscovered the skills my grandmother so patiently taught me.

I was delighted to find that, although a little rusty at first, I hadn't forgotten a thing and, over the last few years, I have spent time honing and expanding my skills. One day, after trying in vain to find a simple, quick and easy design for a bookmark to give my brother, I decided to try designing one myself. This book is the result of those frustrations and my constant desire to produce gifts that are just that little bit different.

129

Index

BOOKS

MAGAZINES

WOODTURNING ◆ WOODCARVING
FURNITURE & CABINETMAKING
THE ROUTER ◆ NEW WOODWORKING
THE DOLLS' HOUSE MAGAZINE
OUTDOOR PHOTOGRAPHY ◆ TRAVEL PHOTOGRAPHY
BLACK & WHITE PHOTOGRAPHY
MACHINE KNITTING NEWS ◆ KNITTING
GUILD OF MASTER CRAFTSMEN NEWS

The above represents a selection of the titles currently
published or scheduled to be published.
All are available direct from the Publishers or through
bookshops, newsagents and specialist retailers.
To place an order, or to obtain a complete catalogue, contact:

**GMC Publications,
Castle Place, 166 High Street, Lewes,
East Sussex BN7 1XU, United Kingdom
Tel: 01273 488005 Fax: 01273 478606
E-mail: pubs@thegmcgroup.com**
Orders by credit card are accepted